Information Privacy Management Practice Exam

By
Majid Hatamian
PhD, CIPM, CIPP/E

ISBN: 9798414431237

Preface

Businesses and organisations across the globe are required to comply with a variety of national and international legislative frameworks designed to protect the rights of individuals. Hence, they have to initiate and manage a set of policies, controls, and strategies to achieve data protection, compliance and governance goals. All these elements can be grouped into a single realm known as *privacy management*. A Certified Information Privacy Manager (CIPM) is a professional that can support an organisation to meet the aforementioned goals and strategies by establishing and managing an efficient information privacy program. As available CIPM practice exams are quite limited (in terms of scope, nature, and availability) and the exam takers may face difficulties to find a reliable source to test their knowledge around information privacy and security management to ensure if they are ready for the actual exam, this book provides you with hands-on experience on privacy, data protection, and governance matters in relation to practical and theoretical aspects of latest technological, legal, governance, and business developments across a privacy program. The *Second Edition* of this book provides a set of 180 multiple-choice and scenario-based questions around fundamental aspects of privacy management such as monitoring and auditing privacy program performance, managing data breaches, privacy awareness training, privacy governance, data protection impact assessments, and many more are carefully designed to profoundly test your existing knowledge on practical and theoretical implications of information privacy management.

How to Use This Book

The *Second Edition* of this book contains 180 questions divided into two practice exams (each exam contains 90 questions). To simulate the situation that you will be likely to experience in the actual CIPM exam, use this book as follows:

Before each practice exam

- Carve out a quiet spot with minimal distractions: This is important to make sure you are not distracted during your practice exam.

- Find an appropriate setting to sit your exam: This may include things like an appropriate chair, desk, a pencil/pen, and a piece of paper.

- Keep an eye on the clock: You may want to set an alarm to remind of the remaining time in your practice exam. Set this for 150 minutes.

- Stay calm: Taking an exam is not always about testing your theoretical and practical knowledge! It is also about your ability to read the questions carefully, formulate what is expected, choose the most appropriate answer, and stay calm if you cannot find the correct answer at first glance. Practising breathing and mindfulness can help a lot.

During each practice exam

- Using the piece of paper and pencil/pen that you already have at hand, write down the number of each question and the most appropriate answer among the available options.

- Flag those questions that you may not be sure about as you may want to review them at the end.

After each practice exam

- Once finished, check the answer chapter for each practice exam where you can find the answer against each question. These chapters are not only providing you with the correct answer for each question, but also a detailed description of why an answer is correct.

- Add up the number of correctly answered questions. If for each exam you would have answered more than 80% of the questions correctly, you might be ready for the actual exam!

If you are also considering to take the CIPT and CIPP/E exams, you may would like to take a look at my other publications entitled *Information Privacy Technologist Practice Exams* and *A Collection of Practice Exams on European Data Protection Law* which are available on Amazon for sale!

As you embark on your privacy and data protection path, I wish you nothing but all the luck and success!

Majid Hatamian

PhD, CIPM, CIPP/E

TABLE OF CONTENTS

Preface   ii

How to Use This Book   iv

CHAPTER

   1. Practice Exam I   1

   2. Practice Exam II   40

   3. Answers for Practice Exam I   72

   4. Answers for Practice Exam II   111

CHAPTER 1

Practice Exam I

1. Setting up a password complexity rule can help an organisation to minimise the risk of which of the following in the first place?

   (a) Social engineering attacks

   (b) Phishing attacks

   (c) Unauthorised access

   (d) Unauthorised data transfer

2. When appointing a Data Protection Officer (DPO) for an organisation, it is important to make sure the DPO:

   (a) Does not receive instructions regarding the exercise of their tasks

   (b) Is certified under a recognised certification scheme

   (c) Is not easily accessible

   (d) Involved in tasks and duties that result in a conflict of interests to the DPO's privacy-related affairs

3. Which one would best match the following definition?

   It is the the ability of an organisation to continue normal operations in the presence of a disruption and recover from that disruption.

   (a) Business continuity

   (b) Business resiliency

   (c) Business strength

   (d) Business tolerance

   Read the following scenario and answer the two follow-up questions:

   Mr. Albertini and Mrs. Weiss submitted a joint mortgage application to Bank ABC. Upon the approval of their application, they purchased a house where they both started to live together. After a while, they decided to leave the original house and each moved to separate addresses. They also informed Bank ABC of this move and their new addresses, accordingly. Acting on its own responsibilities, Bank ABC sent correspondence relating to the mortgage to the old address, where it could be opened by the tenants in situ. Upon noticing this, both Mr. Albertini and Mrs. Weiss decided to lodge a complaint with the respective supervisory authority as they believe their data is mishandled.

4. Which one is correct?

   (a) Mr. Albertini and Mrs. Weiss had to arrange a postal redirect service, so that they could make sure all their mortgage correspondence would be delivered to their new addresses

   (b) The mortgage correspondence would not contain personal data, and therefore, their complaint is not reasonably justified

(c) Bank ABC shall contact the new tenants immediately and ask them to re-direct the mortgage correspondence to Mr. Albertini's and Mrs. Weiss's new addresses

(d) Bank ABC shall stop sending the mortgage correspondence to the Mr. Albertini's and Mrs. Weiss's old address

5. Which one is correct?

(a) Bank ABC has failed to fulfil confidentiality and data accuracy principles

(b) Bank ABC has failed to fulfil confidentiality and data minimisation principles

(c) Bank ABC has fulfilled data accuracy and purpose limitation principles

(d) Bank ABC has fulfilled confidentiality and storage limitation principles

6. Company ABC is using a CCTV system for the security and safety of the workplace. They have established a CCTV policy which states the reason why this system is needed (security and safety). This is also stated on signage in areas where the CCTV cameras are in operation. Company ABC also maintains the CCTV footage on a standalone PC. To ensure a good level of anonymisation, access to CCTV footage is not logged on this PC. One of the employees has been recently dealt with a disciplinary procedure due to his performance in the course of his employment with Company ABC according to the footage captured

by the CCTV system. You have recently joined Company ABC as their Privacy Manager. Which one is the most accurate?

(a) Security and safety is a legitimate purpose on which the Company ABC's use of the CCTV system is based

(b) Company ABC is transparent with regard to its use of the CCTV system as there is a CCTV policy in place

(c) Company ABC's use of anonymisation helps them demonstrate their accountability in line with using appropriate security and organisational measures

(d) The disciplinary procedure against the employee falls within the legitimate purposes on which the company relies

7. Which one is NOT influential for an organisation to evaluate the potential impact on the rights and freedoms of individuals that a privacy incident might cause?

(a) Type of personal data

(b) The origin of the privacy incident

(c) Criticality of the processing operation

(d) Volume of the personal data processed

8. Which one is NOT an example of loss of confidentiality?

(a) A laptop containing personal data is lost during transit

(b) A smartphone is disposed without destroying the personal data

(c) A record that is important for the accuracy of an individual's file in an online healthcare system has been changed

(d) Personal data is mistakenly sent to some unintended recipients

9. Which one is NOT an example of loss of availability in an organisation?

(a) A user database is corrupted and some processing is required to bring the service live again

(b) A customer file is lost and the customers need to provide some information again to the organisation

(c) A database corrupted and there is no back up of this information

(d) A record in an online database has been changed and the individual needs to ask for the service in an offline way

10. Which one might be less likely to result in a threat for an organisation?

(a) An online supermarket offering on-demand deliveries to customers

(b) A Customer Relationship Management system offered through a cloud-based service

(c) A monthly newsletter sent by a church to a subscriber's postal address upon successful subscription in a monthly gathering

(d) A healthcare service provider allowing remote access for its users

11. Which one is NOT an indicator of a poor privacy programme?

(a) Assistants in the accounting unit of a company can enter, modify, and delete data as the same as managers to increase productivity

(b) Hardware and software components are obtained through trusted service providers followed by a formal contractual procedure

(c) Employees are allowed to connect their personal devices to the company's network and infrastructure

(d) No logs of employees accessing the server room of an organisation are kept

12. When it comes to the performance of a privacy programme, what does the term *monitoring* mean?

(a) It relates to all the activities carried out within an organisation to monitor the performance of employees

(b) It relates to all the measures and activities carried out by an organisation to improve the overall satisfaction of its customers in relation to privacy operations

(c) It relates to monitoring the market value of existing privacy-related tools and products

(d) It relates to all the measures in place by an organisation to handle and control privacy management activities and practices

13. Which one is a potential outcome of an efficient privacy programme monitoring?

(a) Improved compliance

(b) Improved revenue

(c) Improved customers' and employees' satisfaction

(d) Improved productivity

14. An employee of your organisation has been recently dismissed. The dismissed employee believes that the dismissal is unfair, and therefore, decides to collect evidence to file an unfair dismissal lawsuit against your organisation. To this end, the employee exercises their right to access to all personal data relating to them. This has been escalated to you as the Privacy Director of the organisation. Which one would be the best course of action in this scenario?

   (a) You will first need to make sure about the intention of the employee. So you will reply to the dismissed employee and inquire about the reason for this data access

   (b) You will only process this access request if the dismissed employee provides you with a reason in advance

   (c) You will process this access request and provide the dismissed employee with all personal data relating to them

   (d) You will refuse this access request because an access request from a dismissed employee is manifestly unfounded or excessive

15. Ms. Garcia works as the staffing manager for Company ABC. As part of her duties, she is responsible for arranging parking spaces for the employees of Company ABC at the company's car park. As the staffing manager of Company ABC, Ms. Garcia has been assigned her own permanent parking space. However, when she arrives at the office after 8am, she notices that her parking space is often already occupied by another car. Since this situation is irritating and repetitive, Ms. Garcia decides to submit a data access request to the organisation

who manages the CCTV system installed in the car park to identify the person who is occupying her parking space. The DPO of the organisation (who manages the CCTV system) is unsure about how to proceed with this request, and therefore, you as the Privacy Director of the organisation are contacted for further advice. What would be your advice in this situation?

(a) Data access is a fundamental privacy right, and therefore, the organisation shall fulfil this request

(b) This data access right might only be fulfilled if Ms. Garcia could prove to the organisation that she had obtained the consent of the employee who was occupying her parking lot

(c) The organisation shall refuse Ms. Garcia's data access request

(d) The organisation shall first check the footage itself to make sure if Ms. Garcia's claim is legit

16. *University U* has made it clear in its privacy notice available on its website that individuals would need to submit any privacy-related queries or concerns in relation to the processing of their personal data to DPO@U.ORG. However, Peter who is an international student at *University U* has sent such a request to SAFETY@U.ORG. He found this email address while he was walking on the premises of the university where he found a notice that says: "Please help us to stop the spread of COVID-19. If you have any questions regarding our safety and sanitary measures, please contact us at SAFETY@U.ORG", which is the e-mail address of the safety staff employed by *University*

U. Which one is correct?

(a) The university shall make all the efforts to make its units and departments aware of such requests, and ask them to immediately forward them to the DPO's contact point

(b) The university shall make sure such requests are automatically redirected to the DPO's contact point and acted upon within the time limits provided by the relevant data protection law

(c) If the safety staff would delay in redirecting this request to the DPO's contact point, then the university is entitled to extend the period for responding to the request, merely because Peter has sent this request to the university's safety staff's e-mail address, and not the university's DPO's contact point

(d) The university is not required to fulfil Peter's request as he has not sent the request to the DPO's contact point

17. Company ABC is a large online marketplace with millions of customers established in the European Economic Area (EEA). The company has fallen victim to a ransomware attack. As a result, the data stored on some of its computers was encrypted by the attacker(s). By getting help from specialised cybersecurity and digital forensics teams and log tracing, Company ABC realises that the attacker(s) only encrypted the data. Thus, no data exfiltration happened (no outward data flow in the timeframe of the attack). Company ABC also found out that the attack only affected the personal data of employees and some customers (42 individuals in total). Moreover, no sensitive personal

data was compromised. Company ABC was able to restore the data from paper backups which took 3 working days and led to minor delays in the delivery of orders to customers. Which one is correct?

 (a) No notification to the respective supervisory authority and affected individuals is needed

 (b) Only notification to the respective supervisory authority is needed

 (c) Only notification to the affected individuals is needed

 (d) Notification to both the respective supervisory authority and affected individuals is needed

18. What types of personal data breaches shall be internally documented?

 (a) Any personal data breaches

 (b) Low risk personal data breaches

 (c) Medium risk personal data breaches

 (d) High risk personal data breaches

19. Which one is NOT an organisational and technical measure for preventing/mitigating the impact of internal human risk sources?

 (a) Disabling print screen function in devices' operating system

 (b) Logging access to sensitive data

 (c) Enabling open cloud services

 (d) Automatically locking all computers after a certain amount of time of inactivity

20. An insurance company receives a phone call from an individual impersonating a client. The individual asks the company to change the postal address to which the billing information should be sent. To fulfil this request, the insurance company validates the client's identity by asking for certain personal data. The individual correctly provides all the requested information. After the validation, the company makes the requested change and the billing information is sent to the new postal address. After a while, the legitimate client contacts the insurance company, inquiring why he is not receiving billing to his postal address any longer, and denies any call from him demanding the change of the postal address. The insurance company notices that the information has been sent to an illegitimate individual and reverts the change. Which one is correct?

    (a) This data breach shall be immediately notified to the competent supervisory authority and the affected individual

    (b) This is not a data breach as the impersonating individual was able to successfully pass the company's identity validation test

    (c) This data breach shall only be internally documented

    (d) This data breach shall be immediately notified only to the competent supervisory authority

21. Chapter V of the GDPR (transfers of personal data to third countries or international organisations) applies to all of the following, except:

    (a) A Swedish insurance company established in Sweden providing personal data of its employees and customers to a company

11

established in Uruguay for further processing on its behalf

(b) A retailer without an EU establishment sending personal data of its employees and customers to a processor for processing in the EU on its behalf

(c) An Estonian cloud service provider acting as the processor of an Austrian bank (established in the EU) delegating a part of the processing activities that it is carrying out on behalf of the bank to a sub-processor established in Vietnam

(d) A person in Germany disclosing personal data to an online jewellery website established in Brazil with no presence in the EU

22. Which one is NOT considered as a data transfer tool for transfers from controllers or processors in the EU/EEA (or otherwise subject to the GDPR) to controllers or processors established outside the EU/EEA (and not subject to the GDPR)?

(a) Administrative arrangements

(b) Binding Corporate Rules

(c) Modernised Standard Contractual Clauses

(d) Old Standard Contractual Clauses

23. What does *full functionality* mean as a privacy-by-design principle?

(a) It indicates the possibility of having strong security and strong privacy

(b) It indicates the necessity of end-to-end security

(c) It indicates the possibility of anticipating and preventing privacy-intrusive events before happening

(d) It indicates the importance of keeping the interests of individuals uppermost

24. From a privacy perspective, the term *trustworthy system* means:

    (a) A system that can be trusted when storing personal data on it

    (b) A system that meets specific security requirements in addition to meeting other critical requirements

    (c) A system that meets specific privacy requirements in addition to meeting other critical requirements

    (d) A system that does not suffer from a privacy breach

25. When carrying out a Data Protection Impact Assessment (DPIA), an organisation shall seek the advice from:

    (a) Competent supervisory authority

    (b) Data Protection Officer (DPO)

    (c) National Security Agency

    (d) Board of directors

26. Which one is less likely to trigger the need for a DPIA?

    (a) Regular and extensive evaluation of individuals' personal sphere

    (b) Processing of small-scale sensitive data such as health data

    (c) Regular monitoring of a publicly accessible area on a large scale

(d) New technologies which are likely to result in high risks

27. Which one is NOT influential in triggering the requirement for conducting a DPIA?

    (a) Number of individuals concerned

    (b) Volume of data being processed

    (c) Geographical location of data processing

    (d) Duration of data processing

28. Which one is NOT likely to trigger the requirement for a DPIA?

    (a) Processing of clients' personal data by a lawyer

    (b) A public authority creating a national fraud database

    (c) Using CCTV to monitor driving behaviour on national roads

    (d) A company enabling its employees to connect with each other via metaverse while working from home to enhance the sense of inclusivity among its employees

29. You are the Privacy Manager of *Sunglass for Fun* (SFF) which is a large business that designs and sells sunglasses with an establishment in Greece. SFF has recently decided to integrate new technologies into its products through the use of augmented reality to provide its customers with an interactive experience of a real-world environment where the objects that reside in the real world are enhanced by computer-generated perceptual information. To get this done, SFF has involved a cloud service provider in the data processing activity to process the live footage captured through the sunglasses' camera to make a unique

profile of its customers' habits. As part of the obligation of SFF under relevant privacy laws, you advise the company to conduct a DPIA to ensure risks are identified and appropriately mitigated or minimised. Which one is correct?

(a) As this is likely to result in high risks, SFF should seek advice from the European Data Protection Board

(b) Cloud service provider is accountable for ensuring that the DPIA is carried out

(c) Both SFF and the cloud service provider are accountable for ensuring that the DPIA is carried out

(d) SFF is accountable for ensuring that the DPIA is carried out

30. A DPIA shall contain all of the following except:

(a) A description of the envisaged processing operations

(b) A description of the purposes of the processing

(c) An assessment of the transparency of the processing

(d) An assessment of the risks to the rights of individuals

31. Which one is correct in relation to the methodology used to carry out a DPIA in an organisation?

(a) The methodology should be sector-specific

(b) The methodology should be approved by a supervisory authority

(c) The methodology should first be approved by a competent supervisory authority and then by the board of directors

(d) The methodology should be sector-generic

32. How does the publication of a DPIA publicly (e.g., on an organisation's website) may impact an organisation?

    (a) Publishing DPIA is a legal requirement which helps an organisation demonstrate compliance with relevant legal frameworks

    (b) Publishing DPIA is not legally required, but it helps increase trust

    (c) Publishing DPIA is not legally required, but an organisation needs to communicate the DPIA to a supervisory authority

    (d) Publishing DPIA is a legal requirement and organisation needs to do so as soon as the outcome of the DPIA is clear

33. An organisation is planning to develop an app for their online marketplace. As part of their privacy programme, they aim at addressing *data minimisation* principle. Which one can help them demonstrate their compliance with this principle?

    (a) Definition and implementation of a data erasure concept

    (b) Preference for automated processes

    (c) Documentation of consents

    (d) Restriction of processing, using and transferring permissions

34. Your organisation has conducted research to identify the possible political origin of tweets circulating on a particularly heated controversy in Austria. For the analysis, your organisation has processed the data of 85,000 Twitter accounts, of which more than 5,400 has been classified

as political. Your organisation is now planning to make the results of this research and its collected dataset publicly available to the general audience. As this research is conducted in Austria, you as the Privacy Director are asked to give advice to the organisation before they make the results of the research and its collected dataset publicly available with regard to potential GDPR implications. What would be your advice in this scenario?

(a) Since the data is collected for research purposes, neither the result nor the collected dataset would trigger GDPR requirements

(b) Neither the results of the research nor its collected dataset can be published as sensitive data is being dealt with

(c) The results of the research and the dataset might be published only if identifiable information is anonymised

(d) The dataset might be published, but not the result of the research as it might discriminate some marginalised groups due to their political views

35. Which one would help an organisation's operational roles to support the practical implementation of privacy and information governance?

(a) Privacy and information governance staff have the authority, support, and resources to carry out their responsibilities effectively

(b) Policies clearly set out the organisational structure for managing privacy and information governance

(c) Privacy and information governance staff understand the organisational structure and their responsibilities

(d) The highest senior management level has overall responsibility for privacy and information governance

36. In a privacy programme, policies and procedures provide the staff of an organisation with enough direction to understand their roles and responsibilities regarding privacy and information governance. Which one is less accurate about such policies and procedures?

(a) Policies and procedures origin from strategic business planning for data protection and information governance

(b) Policies procedures shall cover data protection, records management and information security

(c) Operational procedures, guidance and manuals can help support data protection policies and procedures

(d) As good practice, policies and procedures shall be reviewed at fixed intervals

37. Which one is correct about an organisation's staff privacy training?

(a) The training needs of staff working at the front line of privacy-related matters should be prioritised

(b) The privacy training programme should primarily focus on national-level requirements

(c) The privacy training programme should be regularly reviewed

(d) Regardless of the responsibilities of staff, a holistic privacy training programme should be implemented for all of them

38. Which one is correct about the notion of *privacy policy* and *privacy notice*?

    (a) Privacy policy is always obligatory, but privacy notice is optional

    (b) Privacy policy is an external document aimed at communicating to customers, while privacy notice is an internal document aimed at communicating to staff

    (c) Privacy policy is an internal document aimed at communicating to staff, while privacy notice is an external document aimed at communicating to customers

    (d) They both refer to an organisation's policy concerning privacy breaches

39. What is the goal of *data mapping* in a privacy programme?

    (a) To maximise monetisation based on the collected personal data

    (b) To find out the relation between personal and sensitive data

    (c) To understand what personal data is held and where

    (d) To map the collected personal data to appropriate staff within an organisation

40. Organisations are required to maintain a formal, documented, comprehensive and accurate record of processing activities also referred to as ROPA. Which one is NOT needed to be included in ROPA?

    (a) Description of technical and organisational security measures

    (b) Details of staff privacy training

(c) Name and contact details of the organisation

(d) Purpose(s) of data processing

41. When an organisation relies on consent for personal data processing, which one would be bad practice to ensure consent is validly obtained?

    (a) Consent request is kept separate from other terms and conditions

    (b) Consent request requires a positive opt-out

    (c) Consent request is specific

    (d) Consent request contains the identity of the organisation and the purposes of data processing

42. For a privacy training programme to be effective, it must:

    (a) Be optional for staff

    (b) Be primarily emerged from business needs

    (c) Concern information security and privacy teams

    (d) Be recurrent

Read the following scenario and answer the two follow-up questions:
Company ABC has organised and hosted a social event for its new employees at a city-centre bar. During the social event, an incident involving Employee A and Employee B has taken place and there is an allegation of a serious assault having occurred (assault committed by Employee A on Employee B). The bar has operated a CCTV system on its premises with transparent signage and the incident was fully captured by the CCTV. The incident has been reported by the bar's

manager to the police when they have been called to the premises on the night in question. Furthermore, Company ABC has become aware of the incident and has contacted the bar to verify the reports it has received. The day after the incident, Company ABC has sent its HR officer to the bar to view the CCTV footage on the premises. The HR officer, upon viewing the CCTV footage, considered it a serious incident and requested a copy of the footage so that Company ABC could address the issue. The bar manager allowed the HR officer to take a copy of the footage on their mobile phone as the footage download facility was not working. Employee A has then become aware of this and lodged a complaint with the competent supervisory authority alleging that the bar has disclosed Employee A's personal data, contained in CCTV footage, to his employer without their knowledge or consent.

43. Which one is correct?

    (a) Company ABC obtained the CCTV footage lawfully

    (b) Company ABC obtained the CCTV footage unlawfully, but the bar has collected it lawfully

    (c) Company ABC obtained the CCTV footage unlawfully

    (d) The bar collected the CCTV footage of Employee A unlawfully

44. Which one is correct?

    (a) The bar needed to obtain Employee A's consent before disclosing the CCTV footage to Company ABC

    (b) Company ABC needed to obtain Employee A's consent before obtaining the CCTV footage from the bar

(c) The bar has a legal obligation to disclose the CCTV footage to Company ABC

(d) Company ABC has a legitimate interest to obtain the CCTV footage from the bar

45. Which one is the more likely immediate action upon erroneously sending personal data via e-mail to an unintended recipient?

(a) Acknowledging this to the affected individual

(b) Acknowledging this to the competent supervisory authority

(c) Recalling the e-mail if possible and ask the unintended recipient to confirm they have deleted the e-mail

(d) Acknowledging this to the affected individual and the competent supervisory authority

46. The personal data of a patient including her attendance at the pregnancy unit of a hospital has been disclosed via Facebook messenger by a nurse. Once the patient notices this, she decides to lodge a complaint with the competent supervisory authority. The hospital then claimed to the supervisory authority that the nurse who disclosed the personal data of the patient was in fact employed by a healthcare agency contracted by the hospital. Which one is correct?

(a) The hospital shall address the supervisory authority's concerns

(b) The healthcare agency shall address the supervisory authority's concerns

(c) Facebook messenger uses end-to-end encryption. Thus, appropriate safeguards are in place concerning patient's personal data

(d) Both the hospital and the healthcare agency have to address the supervisory authority's questions and concerns

47. A deaf individual was declined access to services offered by a service provider due to using a sign language interpreter when engaging with the service provider. The service provider referred to privacy concerns as it would not be possible for the service provider to validate the identity of the individual or ensure if the interpreter is indeed acting on behalf of the individual. Which one is correct?

(a) The service provider's decision to refuse the individual's access is lawful

(b) The service provider's decision to refuse the individual's access is unlawful

(c) The service provider's decision to refuse the individual's access is only lawful if the individual could prove that they were deaf

(d) The service provider's decision to refuse the individual's access is only unlawful if the individual could prove that they were deaf

48. Under the GDPR, certification is intended to demonstrate compliance of an organisation in relation to all of the following, except:

(a) Responsibility of the controller (Article 24)

(b) Data protection by design and default (Article 25)

(c) Cooperation with the supervisor authority (Article 31)

(d) Security of processing (Article 32)

49. The structure of an organisation's privacy team is determined by:

    (a) Privacy policies

    (b) Privacy governance model

    (c) Data governance model

    (d) Regulatory requirements

50. Which one is NOT necessary to be included in an organisation's employee privacy policy?

    (a) Statement of the organisation's position

    (b) Statement of the employees' position

    (c) Supplementary information

    (d) Access control measures

51. An appropriate *data mapping* strategy can help develop:

    (a) Efficient data retention and destruction policies

    (b) Appropriate HR policies

    (c) Transparent vendor policies

    (d) A comprehensive list of business needs

52. Which one is a good example of privacy-by-default?

    (a) A mobile app that provides opt-out settings for vice assistant speech recognition functionality

    (b) A website that provides pre-ticked opt-in cookie settings

(c) A browser that disables advertising trackers upon first use

(d) A 'Do Not Track Me' option on a social networking platform

53. You are the Privacy Director of a news media company. The company had reported on the financial difficulties of an individual a long time ago on its website as a result of the economic crisis. Although this information was published a long time ago, they are still accessible on the company's website and indexed in search engines. The individual has recently contacted your company to delete this information. What would be your advice as the Privacy Director of the company?

(a) The news media company is not obliged to address the individual's request

(b) The news media company is obliged to address the individual's request

(c) Both the news media company and search engines are responsible to address the individual's request

(d) The news media company has to address this request only if the search engines do not agree to un-index this information from their search results

54. Which one is NOT a good approach for an organisation when communicating their data processing practices?

(a) Layered interfaces for privacy notices

(b) Alternative formats to present privacy notices

(c) Simplified privacy notices

(d) Using a single channel of communications for information

55. If your organisation is providing services targetted at children, which of the following age categories would be the most likely one that requires greater compliance attention according to the GDPR and COPPA?

    (a) Children under 16 years

    (b) Children under 15 years

    (c) Children under 14 years

    (d) Children under 13 years

56. As part of your organisation's personal data processing activities, you rely on individuals' consent. Which one does NOT need to be included in a consent request?

    (a) The name of your organisation

    (b) The profit that will be generated from the data

    (c) The reason(s) you need the data for

    (d) The purposes for which the data will be processed

57. Which one is incorrect in relation to individuals' access right requests?

    (a) These requests shall always be processed free of charge

    (b) These requests shall always be processed in a timely manner

    (c) These requests shall not adversely affect the rights or freedoms of others

    (d) These requests may include access to health data such as medical records

58. When shaping your organisation's access request policies, is it good practice to implement a *decentralised* intake approach?

   (a) Yes, because a decentralised approach can efficiently distribute the load resulting from these requests among different teams and departments

   (b) Yes, because a decentralised approach enables an organisation to prioritise the use of trained staff when dealing with these requests

   (c) No, because a decentralised approach may impede cooperation among different teams and departments

   (d) No, because a decentralised approach may make it difficult to set an appropriate retention period for these requests

59. Which one is less likely to be good practice to be included in a privacy education and awareness programme within an organisation?

   (a) Developing highly technical programmes

   (b) Developing fun and engaging programmes

   (c) Using real-world case studies to learn from mistakes

   (d) Developing reinforced programmes

60. Which one is NOT deemed to be a good *operational action* in relation to a privacy education and awareness programme in an organisation?

   (a) Communicating information about the planned programme

   (b) Ensuring policies stability

   (c) Designing internal education and awareness programmes

(d) Designing external education and awareness programmes

61. Which one CANNOT be considered as a metric to evaluate the success of a privacy education and awareness training?

    (a) Number of training events completed

    (b) Number of personnel who completed the training events

    (c) Changes to the number of privacy incidents

    (d) Changes to an organisation's revenue

62. Which one would best match the following statement?
    It involves aspects such as process management, security, compliance and software engineering.

    (a) Privacy-by-design

    (b) Privacy engineering

    (c) Security-by-design

    (d) Privacy-enhancing technologies

63. What is the main goal of *corrective* information security controls?

    (a) They help prevent an incident from happening

    (b) They help discover an incident

    (c) They help confine damage resulting from an incident

    (d) They help restrict access to data files

64. Which of the following pair of principles are an example of the overlap between information privacy and information security requirements?

(a) Confidentiality and Availability

(b) Integrity and Confidentiality

(c) Accuracy and Integrity

(d) Data minimisation and Accuracy

65. Which one would best match the following definition as part of Role-Based Access Controls (RBACs)?

   It limits access to data that is necessary to the performance of a task.

   (a) Principle of least privilege

   (b) Need-to-know access

   (c) Segregation of duties

   (d) Remote access service

66. Clean desk policy is an example of:

   (a) Problem escalation procedure

   (b) Security testing

   (c) Risk management

   (d) User access management

67. Which one is correct in relation to the notion of *breach* vs. *incident*?

   (a) All breaches are by default incidents

   (b) All incidents are by default breaches

   (c) Breaches and incidents can be used interchangeably

   (d) Incidents are always more severe than breaches

68. An efficient incident response plan shall consider all, except:

   (a) Integration with business continuity plans

   (b) Appropriate measure to escalate suspicious activities

   (c) Ability to communicate with external stakeholders

   (d) Treating each incident at utmost risk level

69. Which one is correct in relation to Statement A and Statement B regarding an efficient incident response plan?

   Statement A: *During managing an incident, incident response teams shall make sure all staff are duly informed of any progress.*

   Statement B: *Incident response teams shall be given autonomy to confirm legal requirements.*

   (a) Statement A is correct and Statement B is incorrect

   (b) Statement A is incorrect and Statement B is correct

   (c) Both statements are correct

   (d) Both statements are incorrect

70. What does the term *trend analysis* mean in the context of metrics of a privacy programme?

   (a) Identifying patterns when reporting to senior management

   (b) Identifying indicators when measuring return to investment

   (c) Identifying patterns when analysing a privacy programme

   (d) Identifying measures to audit a privacy programme

71. Which one is correct in relation to Statement A and Statement B regarding privacy maturity analysis of an organisation?

Statement A: *Privacy compliance is a journey and progress which is strengthened along the way.*

Statement B: *Privacy programme of an organisation is considered mature when it is at the maximum acceptable level of security.*

   (a) Statement A is correct and Statement B is incorrect

   (b) Statement A is incorrect and Statement B is correct

   (c) Both statements are correct

   (d) Both statements are incorrect

72. The Privacy Maturity Model proposed by the American Institute of Certified Public Accountants (AICPA) and the Canadian Institute of Chartered Accountants (CICA) is based on:

   (a) Generally Accepted Privacy Principles (GAPP)

   (b) The EU's data protection frameworks

   (c) The US's data protection frameworks

   (d) Based on both the EU's and US's data protection frameworks

73. The Privacy Maturity Model (PMM) uses five maturity levels. For an organisation to reach the fifth maturity level:

   (a) It needs to meet all the requirements for previous levels

   (b) It needs to meet all the requirements for levels 1 and 2

   (c) It needs to meet all the requirements for level 4

(d) It can directly start at the fifth level if it could prove that it is not needed to fulfil the requirements for previous levels

74. Which one is correct in relation to Statement A and Statement B regarding the development of the PMM in an organisation?

Statement A: *An organisation shall try to reach the highest achievable level on the maturity model.*

Statement B: *Each organisation's personal information privacy practices may be at various levels.*

(a) Statement A is correct and Statement B is incorrect

(b) Statement A is incorrect and Statement B is correct

(c) Both statements are correct

(d) Both statements are incorrect

75. In developing and calculating an overall maturity level for an organisation under the PMM, the organisation should always:

(a) Determine different weightings to be given to the various criteria

(b) Determine same weightings to be given to all criteria

(c) Follow a simple mathematical average

(d) Document the rationale for weighting each criterion for use in future benchmarking

76. The term *inconsistency* is the keyword for which of the following maturity levels under the PMM?

(a) Repeatable

(b) Defined

(c) Ad hoc

(d) Managed

77. Which one is NOT a form of monitoring in a privacy programme?

    (a) HR monitoring

    (b) Employees career development monitoring

    (c) Data breach monitoring

    (d) Data outsourcing monitoring

78. Your organisation stores personal data of employees and clients in a server room. The organisation has also set up an access control mechanism that registers and maintains the entrance and exit of employees who have the privilege to access the server room. Clear signage has been put in place to make it transparent for employees that the information obtained from this access control mechanism is used to evaluate their performance through monitoring the frequency and exact entrance and exit times of employees. Which one is correct?

    (a) The access control mechanism and its consequent processing is excessive in relation to evaluating the performance of employees

    (b) The access control mechanism and its consequent processing is excessive in relation to securing databases against unauthorised access, loss or theft

    (c) The access control mechanism and its consequent processing is proportionate in relation to evaluating the performance of

33

employees

(d) The access control mechanism and its consequent processing is proportionate in relation to securing databases against unauthorised access as well as evaluating the performance of employees as clear signage has been put in place

79. Company ABC is planning to develop a mobile dating app. Whilst access to the phone's call logs and GPS sensor is not needed for the core functionality of the app, Company ABC is planning to collect this data. To be compliant with transparency obligations, Company ABC is also planning to make this data collection clear in its privacy notice that it will use this data to learn more about the movements and activity levels of its users. However, if a user would decide to withdraw consent at a later point, the dating app would only work to a limited extent. There have been some intense discussions as part of the brainstorming phase among privacy engineers, software engineers, and legal team of Company ABC resulted in some people arguing against/for this idea. This issue is now escalated to you as the Privacy Director of the company. Among the following options, which one would be the most likely scenario to argue against/for this idea?

(a) Consent obtained in this way would be valid, however, degradation of the app's functionality is not justifiable

(b) Consent obtained in this way would be valid and degradation of the app's functionality is justifiable

(c) Consent obtained in this way would be invalid, however, degradation of the app's functionality is justifiable

(d) Consent obtained in this way would be invalid, and thus, any data processing would be unlawful

Read the following scenario and answer the two follow-up questions:
Your organisation maintains an online newsletter. To subscribe to this newsletter, an individual is required to accept the terms of the subscription and contract, which included consent to direct marketing. This also enables your organisation to carry out direct telephone marketing calls using an automated calling system. An easy-to-use opt out mechanism is also brought to the attention of individuals in case they decide to withdraw their consent.

80. Which one is correct in relation to Statement A and Statement B?
Statement A: *The organisation's direct telephone marketing calls using an automated calling system is an example of unsolicited telephone advertising.*
Statement B: *For direct telephone marketing calls using an automated calling system consent is not needed, however, a clear opt out mechanism must be provided to individuals by the organisation.*

(a) Statement A is correct and Statement B is incorrect

(b) Statement A is incorrect and Statement B is correct

(c) Both statements are correct

(d) Both statements are incorrect

81. Which one is correct in relation to Statement A and Statement B?
Statement A: *The organisation obtained individuals' consent invalidly.*

Statement B: *The direct marketing carried out by the organisation is carefully handled because the organisation has obtained consent and provided easy-to-use opt out mechanisms.*

    (a) Statement A is correct and Statement B is incorrect

    (b) Statement A is incorrect and Statement B is correct

    (c) Both statements are correct

    (d) Both statements are incorrect

82. Which one provides individuals with the option to require organisations stop selling their personal data?

    (a) Children's Online Privacy Protection Act (COPPA)

    (b) ePrivacy Directive

    (c) California Consumer Privacy Act (CCPA)

    (d) EU's General Data Protection Regulation (GDPR)

83. Mobile apps' privacy policy notices published by app developers on app markets are an example of:

    (a) On-demand privacy notice

    (b) At-setup privacy notice

    (c) Context-dependent privacy notice

    (d) Just-in-time privacy notice

84. The successful execution of a privacy programme in an organisation is the main responsibility of:

(a) Legal department

(b) All staff

(c) Legal and IT departments

(d) The board of directors

85. An organisation has placed redundant servers at its premises. By doing so, which of the following security controls is addressed?

(a) Detective

(b) Preventative

(c) Obstructive

(d) Corrective

86. An organisation that has policies and procedures to ensure data protection issues are considered when systems, services, products and business practices involving personal data are designed and implemented is trying to address:

(a) Privacy engineering

(b) Privacy-by-design

(c) Cybersecurity attacks

(d) Privacy maturity model

87. Availability as an information security principle is more likely to be affected by which of the following cyber attacks?

(a) Malware

(b) Ransomware

(c) Spyware

(d) Sniffing

88. If the initial analysis of a proposed personal data processing activity indicates no need for a DPIA, then:

(a) This should be documented

(b) This should not be documented

(c) This should be only documented if approval from DPO is obtained

(d) This should not be documented unless sensitive data is involved

89. Your organisation deals with health data of patients. As a result, it needs to comply with HIPAA which requires specific safeguards regarding data confidentiality and encryption. Recently, your organisation has fallen victim to a cyber attack that has allowed attackers to decrypt the encrypted health data stored on your organisation's storage and infiltrate this data to an unknown server. The attack indicates that your organisation has failed to safeguard health data:

(a) In-transit

(b) At-rest

(c) In-use

(d) In-motion

90. What is the goal of data governance in an organisation?

(a) Data governance focuses on the technical aspects of data processing such as data security

(b) Data governance focuses on the organisational aspects of data processing such as data policies and compliance

(c) Data governance focuses on both technical and organisational aspects of data processing

(d) Data governance focuses on risk management

CHAPTER 2

Practice Exam II

1. All of the following are examples of information that need to be included in a DPIA, except:

   (a) Context and purposes of data processing

   (b) Necessity and proportionality

   (c) Risks to the business

   (d) Measures to mitigate risks

2. An organisation is planning to run a privacy governance programme. Which one is more likely to be the first step to be taken?

   (a) Hiring a Chief Privacy Officer

   (b) Purchasing technical and organisational equipment such as information governance software

   (c) Establishing vendor security assessment procedures

   (d) Conducting an assessment of business and compliance needs

3. Which one is correct in relation to appointing a DPO?

   (a) DPO shall never receive instructions regarding the exercise of their tasks except from the regulatory bodies

   (b) DPO can only receive instructions regarding the exercise of their tasks from senior management

   (c) DPO can only receive instructions regarding the exercise of their tasks from the CEO

   (d) DPO shall never receive instructions regarding the exercise of their tasks

4. A laptop containing personal data is lost. This is an example of:

   (a) Loss of Integrity

   (b) Loss of Confidentiality

   (c) Loss of Accountability

   (d) Loss of Proportionality

5. A database corrupted and there is no back up of this information. This is an example of loss of:

   (a) Accuracy

   (b) Availability

   (c) Integrity

   (d) Confidentiality

6. Which one is NOT a risk resulted from the Bring Your Own Device (BYOD) policy within an organisation?

(a) Decreased device management

(b) Increased data theft

(c) Increased productivity

(d) Decreased data vetting

7. What is the objective of *Preventative not Remedial* as one of the principles of privacy-by-design?

    (a) Ensures data is securely collected, processed, stored and destroyed

    (b) Ensures privacy-intrusive events are anticipated before they occur

    (c) Ensuring the interest of individuals is kept uppermost

    (d) Ensuring both strong security and strong privacy

8. Privacy risk responses deal with negative consequences of a privacy risk. Which one is NOT one of the four privacy risk responses?

    (a) Risk transfer

    (b) Risk acceptance

    (c) Risk mitigation

    (d) Risk extension

9. It is unavoidable for an organisation to establish an appropriate incident management plan. Which one can be achieved by an organisation's investment in planning and improving its incident management?

    (a) Reduced time response and recovery actions

    (b) Increased impact on day-to-day services

(c) Reduced productivity

(d) Increased compliance issues

10. An organisation has informal risk management practices accompanied with reactive security risk controls. Which of the following levels of the Privacy Maturity Model (PMM) is more likely to describe the organisation's view on risk management?

   (a) Ad hoc

   (b) Repeatable

   (c) Defined

   (d) Managed

11. Privacy and security controls can help an organisation meet compliance requirements. An organisation has decided to withdraw some of the already implemented controls. Which one is NOT a good reason to withdraw privacy and security controls?

   (a) Capability offered by the control is incorporated into another control

   (b) Control is redundant to an existing control

   (c) Control is causing high implementation costs

   (d) Control is deemed to be no longer necessary

12. As part of account management policies of an organisation, the organisation decides to disable expired accounts. Which of the following principles is most likely to be met by this policy?

(a) Need-to-know access

(b) Least privilege

(c) Remote access service

(d) Segregation of duties

13. Insufficient attention to which of the following can adversely affect an organisation's capability to carry out its business functions?

    (a) Trustworthiness of IT products and systems

    (b) Reliability of IT products and systems

    (c) Productivity of IT products and systems

    (d) Affordability of IT products and systems

14. Which one is NOT primarily an objective of an Acceptable Use Policy (AUP)?

    (a) Promoting compliance in relation to the use of systems

    (b) Restricting the ways in which systems and services may be used

    (c) Establishing guidelines on how systems and services shall be used

    (d) Stipulating sanctions in relation to the use of systems and services

15. Which one is an example *something you are* authentication factor?

    (a) Passwords

    (b) RFID

    (c) Location

    (d) Retinal scan

16. A city council offers a chip card to regular users of the public transport system for a certain fee. The name of the users is printed on the card's surface which is also stored electronically in the chip. When a user uses the public transport system, e.g., the tram, the card must touch the reading terminal already installed in the tram. The data read by the terminal is electronically checked against a database containing the names of the users who have bought the travel card. Which of the following privacy principles is NOT respected in this scenario?

    (a) Accountability

    (b) Data minimisation

    (c) Confidentiality

    (d) Lawfulness, fairness and transparency

17. Which one is NOT a preventative control?

    (a) Weekly analysis of an organisation's transactions

    (b) Employee screening and training

    (c) Locks on doors

    (d) Passwords

Read the following scenario and answer the two follow-up questions:
Company ABC is a large European-based green energy supplier with more than 65,000 employees and reported annual sales of 10 billion (Euro). In September 2018, the company suffered from a ransomware attack that affected some of the servers supporting its non-European IT systems. The company suspended all affected systems, then contacted

law enforcement. Investigations into the attack revealed that data exfiltration started after leaked credentials were exploited as far back as January 2018. The attack did not affect Company ABC's backup data or core systems. Hence, the company was able to recover from the attack in a few days with minimal disruption to the supply chain. Moreover, to further minimize the risk of sensitive stolen data being published online, Company ABC decided to pay a ransom of 5 million (Euro) to attackers.

18. Which one is most likely to intensify the severity of this attack?

    (a) Declining to pay the ransom

    (b) Failing to involve law enforcement

    (c) Failing to suspend affected systems

    (d) Lack of back up data

19. Which one could potentially prevent this attack?

    (a) Enforcing strong authentication policies

    (b) Regular cybersecurity awareness trainings for employees

    (c) Efficient incident response plan

    (d) Early incident detection

20. This security objective aims at safeguarding against improper information modification or destruction and ensuring information non-repudiation and authenticity. Which one best matches this definition?

    (a) Confidentiality

(b) Availability

(c) Manageability

(d) Integrity

21. This concept allows an organisation to iteratively assess privacy controls for their effectiveness in meeting the privacy requirements and managing privacy risks. Which one best matches this concept?

(a) Privacy requirements engineering

(b) Privacy governance programme

(c) Privacy requirements traceability

(d) Privacy controls governance

22. Company ABC uses an access control method in which employees can only access the information needed to perform their duties. Which one best matches this access control method?

(a) Policy-based access control

(b) Role-based access control

(c) Attribute-based access control

(d) Rule-based access control

23. Which one is an example of privacy risk avoidance?

(a) A dating app asking if the user is above 18

(b) An online shop relying on contractual agreements when involving third party vendors in personal data processing of their customers

(c) A bank taking hourly backup from their customers data

(d) A company using encryption when storing personal data of users

24. Which one is correct about *authentication* and *authorisation*?

   (a) Both are examples of privacy-by-design

   (b) Both are used to encrypt data

   (c) Authentication is about verifying what a user can have access to, while authorisation is about verifying their identity

   (d) Authentication is about verifying who a user is, while authorisation is about verifying what they have access to

25. Which one is NOT a detective control?

   (a) Weekly monitoring of organisational transactions

   (b) Access controls

   (c) Physical inventories

   (d) Review organisational performance

26. Company ABC provides team collaboration tools to organisations globally. A few days ago, one of the company's legacy tools was compromised with multiple zero-day vulnerabilities exploited by ransomware hackers. As a result of the attack, several other vendors who were relying on collaboration tools offered by Company ABC were also affected. Which one is most likely to prevent this attack?

   (a) Regular cybersecurity awareness trainings for employees

(b) Using risk-based vulnerability management tools to prioritize patch assets

(c) Applying deep packet inspection techniques to malicious traffic impacting the vendors

(d) Enforcing strong authentication policies to safeguard networks and systems from unauthorised access

27. What is the difference between Role-Based (RB) and Policy-Based (PB) access controls?

(a) RB is based on allowing users access to resources depending on rules, whereas PB does the same depending users' roles

(b) RB is based on allowing users access to resources depending on their roles, whereas PB does the same depending on rules

(c) RB is based on allowing users access to resources depending on their attributes, whereas PB does the same depending on rules

(d) RB is based on allowing users access to resources depending on their roles, whereas PB does the same depending on users' attributes

28. A company is only allowing its HR department employees to read and write PDF, JPEG, and PNG files from the server rooms. Which one best matches this access control method?

(a) Policy-based access control

(b) Role-based access control

(c) Attribute-based access control

(d) Rule-based access control

29. Which one is NOT a benefit of privacy risk assessment?

    (a) Identifying privacy risks

    (b) Prioritising privacy risks

    (c) Avoiding scrutiny

    (d) Demonstrating compliance

30. Which one is NOT a good source of deriving organisational-level privacy requirements?

    (a) Legal environment

    (b) Organisational policies

    (c) Expert opinions

    (d) Privacy principles

31. Which one is NOT an appropriate response to a privacy risk?

    (a) Evolving the risk

    (b) Mitigating the risk

    (c) Transferring the risk

    (d) Accepting the risk

32. Which of the following roles in an organisation is less likely to conflict with a DPO's responsibilities?

    (a) A person who defines IT strategy in an organisation, including where the data resides, accessed by who and how and what infrastructure to use

(b) A person who creates security strategies with certain prioritisations in an organisation

(c) A person who balances the interests of their organisation against what is permissible and/or possible under applicable law

(d) A person who analyses and checks the compliance of processing activities in an organisation

33. Which one is correct in relation to *data governance* and *information governance*?

(a) Data governance deals with organisational aspects of data processing, while information governance deals with technical aspects

(b) They both focus on technical aspects of data processing

(c) They both focus on organisational aspects of data processing

(d) Data governance is a subset of information governance

34. One of the vendors that your organisation is working with has recently fallen victim to a privacy breach which is likely to impact your day-to-day business. What would you recommend to this organisation as an immediate action?

(a) Require all your employees to change their passwords

(b) Make sure that the vendor takes steps to remedy the breach

(c) Do not allow employees to use their personal devices when connected to organisation's networks

(d) Notify the breach to a supervisory authority

35. Company ABC has designed a privacy governance programme with the aim to collect, process, and store the minimum required amount of personal data. Which one is the more likely concept that this company is trying to incorporate in its privacy governance programme?

   (a) Privacy engineering

   (b) Privacy-by-default

   (c) Privacy-by-design

   (d) Security-by-design

36. Which one is more likely to be the first step in protecting personal data across an organisation?

   (a) Creating data inventory policies and procedures

   (b) Ensuring end-to-end encryption for any personal data transfers

   (c) Establishing strict access controls and passwords for personal data storages

   (d) Addressing privacy law requirements

37. You are acting as the Privacy Manager of an organisation. Your organisation is going to be engaged in a data processing activity that involves three other vendors that may be likely to access personal data of customers collected by your organisation. In order to minimise the risk of these vendors accessing personal data, you recommend your organisation to apply encryption techniques to the personal data shared with these vendors, so that data can remain confidential while it

is used and processed by the vendors. Which of the following concepts is the more likely outcome of implementing your recommendation?

(a) Protecting data in-use

(b) Protecting data at-rest

(c) Protecting data in-transit

(d) Protecting data end-to-end

38. Which one is NOT a type of privacy governance model?

(a) Centralised

(b) Decentralised

(c) Operationalised

(d) Local

39. As part of creating a work-from-anywhere (WFA) security policy in relation to remote-working of employees, an organisation should:

(a) Follow best industry practices

(b) Make its own risk-based decisions

(c) Abolish the WFA policy when organisation's devices are not used

(d) Limit the WFA to senior management only

40. Which one is more likely to mitigate the risk resulted from employees' insecure personal devices connected to an organisation's network?

(a) Creating a separate network within the organisation dedicated to personal devices

(b) Regularly updating network intrusion systems

(c) Running cybersecurity awareness campaigns to increase employees' awareness of using insecure devices

(d) Blocking access to networks by insecure devices

41. Which one is NOT a recommended practice for a password policy?

(a) Enforcing sufficiently long passwords

(b) Enforcing complex passwords

(c) Enforcing password hints

(d) Disallowing the use of same passwords for multiple accounts

42. Account management is an important aspects of a privacy programme. Which of the following tasks is less likely to require an administrative account (an administrative account is an account with full privileges)?

(a) Installing software and OS updates

(b) Managing employees accounts

(c) Adjusting server settings

(d) Using an email client software

43. Which one is an example of an unauthorised physical access threat?

(a) An employee's laptop is left unattended in the conference room

(b) An employee using a public Wi-Fi to access an organisation's resources

(c) An employee using an illegal software

(d) An employee using an unknown VPN while connected to an organisation's network

44. An organisation's policies and processes shall make sure that personal data sharing decisions are handled appropriately. Which one is NOT deemed as an effective way to ensure personal data sharing decisions are handled appropriately?

    (a) Personal data sharing decisions are made based on consent

    (b) Review processes such as DPIAs

    (c) Documenting sharing decisions

    (d) Employees involved in personal data sharing decisions receive appropriate training

45. Which one is NOT good practice when involving parties with whom an organisation regularly shares personal data?

    (a) Creating a detailed data sharing agreement

    (b) Setting out responsibilities in case a privacy breach happens

    (c) Regularly reviewing the agreement to ensure its relevancy

    (d) Setting up a directory mainly of active data sharing agreements

46. Which one is NOT relevant when completing a DPIA?

    (a) Establishing procedures to decide if a DPIA is needed

    (b) Incorporating senior-level managers' advice in the DPIA

    (c) Documenting the DPIA as to whether it is needed or not

    (d) Training staff who are involved in conducting the DPIA

47. All of the following are examples of due diligence carried out by an organisation when engaging a vendor in personal data sharing, except:

   (a) The risk of the processing

   (b) Site visits

   (c) Inspections at fixed intervals

   (d) Audit requests

48. When transferring data off an organisation, all of the following are examples of appropriate measures, except:

   (a) Creating contracts for data transfers

   (b) Documenting both digital and physical (e.g., post) data transfers

   (c) Using a secure public network

   (d) Following a risk-based approach

49. What does the term *data quality* mean in a privacy programme?

   (a) Data quality ensures personal data is not excessive

   (b) Data quality ensures personal data is of good business quality

   (c) Data quality determines how diverse personal data types are

   (d) Data quality ensures confidentiality

50. A data retention policy outlines storage periods for personal data held by an organisation. Which one is NOT an indicator of an efficient data retention policy?

   (a) Automating retention processes when the retention period expires

(b) Establishing retention policies merely based on statutory needs

(c) Regularly evaluating the retained data to explore opportunities for anonymisation

(d) Assigning responsibilities to dedicated employees to adhere to the retention period

51. Which one does NOT help against unauthorised access to an organisation's resources?

(a) Setting up maximum password complexity rules

(b) Limiting log on attempts to systems

(c) Regularly updating software tools

(d) Using intrusion detection techniques

52. An organisation is planning to update its transparency procedures. Which one would best help them avoid the integration of the so-called *privacy dark patterns*?

(a) A big pop-up window informing an individual to read the privacy notice of the organisation's website upon the first visit, while the 'Close This Window' button is much smaller

(b) A small pop-up window informing an individual to read the privacy notice of the organisation's website upon the first visit, while the 'Close This Window' button is much bigger

(c) A pre-checked opt-in cookie settings upon visiting the organisation's website for the first time

(d) Showing countdowns to an individual upon visiting the organisation's website for the first time to accept the terms and conditions

53. Allowing employees to take devices, data or software off the premises of an organisation without prior authorisation is an example of:

(a) Inappropriate DPIA

(b) Inappropriate physical security policy

(c) Inappropriate data inventory

(d) Inappropriate remote/home working policy

54. In the context of a privacy governance programme, the term *business continuity* refers to the ability of an organisation to:

(a) Recover from a disruption

(b) Maintain operations despite an unexpected disruption

(c) Maintain operations despite an expected disruption

(d) Maintain operations despite any disruptions

55. An organisation has recently received a data access request from an individual. Soon after receiving this request, the organisation notices that the individual has a job application for a vacancy within this organisation that has been stored beyond the retention period. Which one would be the best course of action when replying to the data access request submitted by the individual?

(a) The organisation shall grant data access first and then delete the job application data

(b) The organisation shall delete the job application data first and then grant data access

(c) The organisation shall continue storing the job application and notify the individual

(d) The organisation shall ask for advice from a supervisory authority

56. Most privacy laws require organisations to notify privacy breaches to relevant supervisory authorities when they are likely to result in high risks to individuals within a certain time-frame. In the likely event of a high risk privacy breach, when does an organisation need to notify a relevant supervisory authority?

(a) Upon staring the investigation into the breach

(b) Upon successful recovery from the breach

(c) Upon becoming aware of the breach

(d) Once upon becoming aware of the breach and once upon successful recovery

57. Which one is NOT an effective privacy notice communication?

(a) Having a free and easily locatable privacy notice

(b) Using a single-mode of communication

(c) Providing privacy notice in hard-copy and digital formats

(d) Using simple language when targetting children

58. Mobile apps' permission pop-ups upon installation are an example of:

(a) On-demand privacy notice

(b) At-setup privacy notice

(c) Context-dependent privacy notice

(d) Just-in-time privacy notice

59. Under the EU GDPR, an organisation is required to maintain a repository containing information about any data processing activity that they carry out such as records of consent, types of personal data collected and retained, retention period and more. What is the name of this repository?

(a) Logs of processing activities

(b) Record of processing activities

(c) Data protection impact assessment

(d) Consent management software

60. This attack targets organisations by encouraging employees to open links or email attachments. Which one would best match this attack?

(a) Ransomware

(b) Denial of service

(c) Network intrusion

(d) Phishing

61. Which one is NOT influential when deciding on the impact of a cyber attack on an organisation?

(a) Affected data types

(b) Number of impacted customers

(c) Location of the attacker

(d) Availability of services

62. Which one is less likely to be the cause of a cyber incident?

   (a) Complex credentials

   (b) Human mistakes

   (c) Disgruntled employees

   (d) System vulnerabilities

63. Which one is correct in relation to an incident response plan (IRP)?

   (a) IRP involves multiple stakeholders within an organisation

   (b) Legal department is often responsible for an IRP

   (c) Legal and IT departments are often responsible for an IRP

   (d) An IRP always needs an approval from an independent authority

64. Which of the following information security principles is likely to be more severely affected than others by a ransomware attack?

   (a) Confidentiality

   (b) Integrity

   (c) Availability

   (d) Accuracy

65. An effective staff privacy training shall cover all the following except:

   (a) Indefinite timescales

(b) Staff training needs

(c) Trainers needs

(d) Dedicated resources

66. Company ABC has fallen victim to a ransomware attack. After careful investigations, the company confirms that no personal data has been uploaded or leaked from their servers. Which one is more accurate?

    (a) This may be considered as a personal data breach

    (b) This may be considered as a security incident, but not a personal data breach

    (c) This may be considered both as a security incident and a personal data breach

    (d) This is neither a security incident nor a personal data breach

67. In testing and assessing security controls implemented as part of an incident response plan, which one is less likely to be of relevance?

    (a) Disaster recovery

    (b) Breach notification

    (c) Software testing

    (d) HR management

68. Company ABC has been recently hacked. The attack has resulted in the theft of email addresses and hashed passwords of approximately 10 million users. After a while, most of these email addresses and passwords were published online by the attackers. Which one is a more likely threat resulted from this attack?

(a) Phishing

(b) Identity theft

(c) Malware

(d) Denial of service

69. Which one is NOT influential when deciding on the implementation of technical and organisation measures to address privacy and security risks within an organisations?

(a) Risk likelihood

(b) Cost of implementation

(c) Cost of fines

(d) Risk severity

70. Which one is more appropriate to ensure explicit consent is obtained from the user of a website?

(a) "It is clear to me that my personal data will be processed"

(b) "I understand that my personal data will be processed by continuing using this service"

(c) "I, hereby, consent to the processing of my personal data"

(d) "You understand that by providing your personal data, we will use them to recommend appropriate healthy products"

71. Which one is NOT one of the four well-known authentication factors?

(a) What you are

(b) What you have

(c) What you share

(d) Where you are

72. As part of the considerations for designing usable privacy interfaces and notices for users, the main attention should be given to addressing:

(a) Compliance requirements

(b) User requirements

(c) Business requirements

(d) Technology requirements

Read the following scenario and answer the two follow-up questions: *Company ABC is a nation-wide gasoline transport company. Few months ago, a ransomware attacker managed to infiltrate Company ABC's billing system. As a result, the company stopped all pipeline operations to contain the attack. The disruption lasted five days while Company ABC responded to the incident. Part of the response involved paying a 8.4 million (US Dollar) ransom to the attacker. The concern around this breach was elevated by media images of panicked people queueing in front of gas stations as a result of fearing an extended fuel shortage. Further investigations into the cyber attack on Company ABC found that the initial attack vector was a breached password used to log into the company's VPN. It was further revealed that the company failed to mandate their employees to use strong passwords.*

73. Which one is more likely to prevent this attack?

(a) Having daily server back-up

(b) Using a two-hop VPN

(c) Using multi-factor authentication

(d) Enforcing strong password policies

74. All of the following are correct, except:

    (a) Company ABC uses poor password hygiene policy

    (b) The attack shows that Company ABC needs to improve its workforce cyber awareness and training programme

    (c) An antivirus installed on the company's VPN could potentially prevent this attack

    (d) The attack shows that Company ABC needs to improve its incident monitoring programme

75. What is the main goal of a phishing simulation campaign?

    (a) To anticipate phishing attacks

    (b) To determine which employees should be promoted

    (c) To evaluate the effectiveness of security awareness training

    (d) To shame users who failed the phishing test

76. In August 2016, a large European health service provider suffered from a ransomware attack which resulted in healthcare professionals losing access to IT systems, including patient information and laboratory systems. Investigations into this attack revealed that the attack started in February 2016 when an employee opened a malicious email

attachment. This attachment provided remote access to the health service provider's IT infrastructure. This allowed attackers to use a penetration testing tool to escalate their privileges on the originally compromised workstation. The health service provider had to pay 1 million (Euro) ransom to the attacker. Which one is more accurate?

(a) The health service provider should stop paying ransom for similar attacks and prepare an efficient incident response plan

(b) The health service provider should establish a dedicated team of digital forensic investigators to expedite investigation in the likely event of future attacks

(c) The health service provider should assign a DPO to escalate similar incidents to a supervisory authority

(d) The health service provider should use efficient intrusion detection systems and revise its employee cybersecurity awareness programme

77. This technique allows an organisation to remove the association between a database and an individual. What is this technique?

(a) Normalization

(b) Pseudonymization

(c) Anonymization

(d) Re-identification

78. Which one is NOT influential when designing understandable consent choices for children?

(a) Timing

(b) Regulatory needs

(c) Age

(d) Presentation

79. Under the Health Insurance Portability and Accountability Act (HIPAA), an organisation has to respond to an individual's request for access to their data no later than:

(a) 28 days

(b) 30 days

(c) 60 days

(d) 90 days

80. Which one is correct in relation to the California Privacy Right Act (CPRA) and the California Consumer Privacy Act (CCPA)?

(a) Both recognise the right to data rectification

(b) Both recognise the right to reject automated decision making

(c) CPRA mandates the appointment of DPO, while CCPA does not

(d) CPRA recognises the right to the restriction of sensitive data usage, while CCPA does not

81. Which one is more accurate in relation to steps taken by an organisation when selecting vendors who will have access to sensitive data?

(a) Always doing business with well-known vendors

(b) Ensuring vendors understand compliance rules

(c) Establishing provisions in vendor contracts to examine and revise privacy and security controls

(d) Confirming that vendors understand the importance of privacy and security controls

82. Which one is correct in relation to Statement A and Statement B? Statement A: *The EU GDPR recognises the right to data portability.* Statement B: *The EU GDPR recognises the right to not be subject to automated decision making.*

(a) Statement A is correct and Statement B is incorrect

(b) Statement A is incorrect and Statement B is correct

(c) Both statements are correct

(d) Both statements are incorrect

83. Which one is correct about *Data Subject Access Right* (DSAR)?

(a) Always one copy of personal data can be provided to individuals upon exercising this right

(b) Organisations should ensure this right does affect the rights of others

(c) Not all individuals whose personal data is held by organisations are entitled to this right

(d) It guarantees access to personal data held by an organisation about an individual

84. Which one is incorrect regarding the term *processor* under the GDPR?

   (a) A processor is a natural or legal person that processes personal data on behalf of a controller

   (b) A processor becomes a controller if it determines the means and purposes of data processing itself

   (c) The processor may only engage a sub-processor in data processing activities subject to specific or general written authorisation of the controller

   (d) If the sub-processor fails to fulfil its data protection obligations, the sub-processor is fully liable to the controller

85. Which one does NOT refer to the data minimisation principle?

   (a) Data processing must be limited to what is necessary to fulfil a legitimate purpose

   (b) Processing of personal data should only take place when the purpose of processing cannot be fulfilled by other means

   (c) Data processing may not disproportionately interfere with the interests, rights and freedoms of the individual

   (d) Any processing of personal data must be done for a specific well-defined purpose

86. Which one is more likely to go against the purpose limitation principle when processing personal data of individuals?

   (a) A lawyer discloses her customers list to her husband, who owns a restaurant nearby the law firm, so that they can offer special meal offers when customers visiting the law firm

(b) A recruitment agency places workers in a variety of jobs and sends applicants a general questionnaire, which includes specific questions about health conditions that are only relevant to particular manual occupations

(c) An employer receives several applications for a job vacancy and keeps the recruitment records for unsuccessful applicants beyond the statutory period

(d) As a remedy against potential ransomware attacks, an organisation plans to take regular backups of its systems and the personal data stored on them

87. A health service provider collects data about blood groups of some of its staff who do hazardous work. This data is needed just in case an accident occurs at work even though the appropriate safety measures are in place to ensure a safe workplace for all the staff. The health service provider needs to store this data in compliance with labour law. Which of the following principles is the health service provider more likely trying to address?

(a) Purpose limitation

(b) Storage limitation

(c) Data minimisation

(d) Confidentiality and integrity

88. A credit agency maintains a database containing data on the credit history of individuals to check their creditworthiness. Failure to adhere

to which of the following principles is more likely to result in unfair treatment of an individual when submitting credit applications?

(a) Data minimisation

(b) Storage limitation

(c) Data accuracy

(d) Transparency

89. What is the goal of the Privacy Maturity Model (PMM)?

(a) To address privacy risks

(b) To assess the progress of a privacy programme

(c) To respond to individuals' requests

(d) To monitor compliance with privacy laws

90. Which one is less likely to be an efficient metric when monitoring the overall progress of a privacy programme within an organisation?

(a) Number of personal data breaches

(b) The rate of consent for personal data sharing

(c) Number of signed transfer impact assessments

(d) Number of meetings held by privacy teams

CHAPTER 3

Answers for Practice Exam I

Answer Key for Practice Exam I

Q	A	Q	A	Q	A	Q	A	Q	A
1	c	19	c	37	c	55	d	73	a
2	a	20	a	38	c	56	b	74	b
3	b	21	d	39	c	57	a	75	d
4	d	22	d	40	b	58	c	76	c
5	a	23	a	41	b	59	a	77	b
6	a	24	c	42	d	60	b	78	a
7	b	25	b	43	a	61	d	79	d
8	c	26	b	44	d	62	b	80	a
9	d	27	c	45	c	63	c	81	a
10	c	28	a	46	a	64	c	82	c
11	b	29	d	47	b	65	b	83	a
12	d	30	c	48	c	66	d	84	b
13	a	31	a	49	b	67	a	85	d
14	c	32	b	50	b	68	d	86	b
15	c	33	b	51	a	69	d	87	b
16	d	34	c	52	c	70	c	88	a
17	b	35	a	53	a	71	a	89	b
18	a	36	d	54	d	72	a	90	a

Detailed Answers for Practice Exam I

1. Answer: (c)

   Passwords can protect an organisation's resources from unauthorised access. Enforcing a password complexity policy can help an organisation minimise the risk of unauthorised access to resources and services. Note that a password complexity policy can prevent unauthorised access in the first place (unauthorised access itself may result in authorised data transfers).

2. Answer: (a)

   (a) is correct, because it is vital for every organisation to make sure that the DPO does not receive any instructions regarding the exercise of their tasks. Moreover, organisations shall make sure the DPO's tasks and responsibilities do not result in a conflict of interests with their privacy-related tasks and duties.

3. Answer: (b)

   Business continuity refers to the ability of an organisation to maintain normal operations following any disruptions (e.g., a security incident). Business resiliency is a more broader term than business continuity that encompasses both continuity and recovery aspects of a business following a disruption.

4. Answer: (d)

   In this scenario, the organisation (Bank ABC) has failed to follow its data accuracy responsibilities. The data in question consisted of (amongst other things) financial information relating to the mortgage.

Hence, the data is personal data because it relates to Mr. Albertini and Mrs. Weiss as individuals, and therefore, they could be identified from it. Thus, (b) is incorrect. Obviously, (a) and (c) are incorrect as well, as this is not Mr. Albertini's and Mrs. Weiss's responsibility to arrange a re-direct service (although they could if they wished), as they had already informed the organisation (Bank ABC) of their new addresses. Similarly, it is not the new tenants' responsibility to initiate a re-direct service for Mr. Albertini and Mrs. Weiss.

5. Answer: (a)

Accuracy and confidentiality are two important privacy principles. Accuracy requires organisations to ensure personal data is accurate and kept up to date where necessary. Confidentiality requires organisations to implement appropriate technical and organisational measures to safeguard personal data. In this scenario, Bank ABC failed to keep Mr. Albertini's and Mrs. Weiss's personal data up to date. Moreover, given that the mortgage correspondence was being sent to the old address, it is clear that Bank ABC's security measures failed to appropriately safeguard Mr. Albertini's and Mrs. Weiss's personal data. Therefore, the correct answer is (a).

6. Answer: (a)

(b) is incorrect, because the employee's personal data (biometric data captured using the CCTV system) was initially collected for security and safety reasons which is also reflected in company's CCTV policy. However, the CCTV policy does not indicate whether such data is going to be used for any other purposes than the initial one (security and safety). Later on, this data was used to monitor the employee's performance in the course of his employment with Company ABC, and therefore, Company ABC is clearly not transparent with regard to its data processing activities concerning the use of the CCTV system. Where personal data is processed for a purpose that is different from the one for which it was collected, the purposes underlying such further processing must not be incompatible with the original purposes. In relation to the use of the employee's personal data, the purpose of monitoring their performance was separate and distinct from the original purpose of security and safety for which the CCTV footage was collected. On that basis, the processing of the employee's personal data contained in the CCTV footage for the purpose of monitoring performance was further processing for a purpose that was incompatible with the original purposes of its collection. (c) is incorrect, because the absence of an access log for the CCTV footage is a deficiency in data security controls in general (which cannot be deemed as anonymisation which is a completely different concept) which is going against the obligation for organisations to implement appropriate security and organisational measures. (d) is incorrect, because while the personal data (footage) captured from the CCTV system might be used for a legitimate purpose (security and safety), it is not well-justified to rely on such an intrusive data processing operation to evaluate the performance of employees and bring disciplinary procedures against them.

7. Answer: (b)

(a) is incorrect, because the type of personal data is influential when evaluating the impact of a privacy incident. For instance, when data includes medical records or information on religious beliefs, the impact of a privacy breach can be severe on the individuals. (c) is incorrect, because criticality (e.g., systematic tracking, monitoring or surveillance of individuals) of the data processing might be influential when deciding on the impact of a privacy incident. Similarly, (d) is incorrect, because the more personal data would be processed, the more impactful the privacy incident might be. For instance, in case of a privacy breach at the servers of a social media provider, the impact on an individual might be higher if this data would cover a period of two years rather than two weeks.

8. Answer: (c)

   All the other options are examples of loss of confidentiality, while (c) is an example of loss of integrity.

9. Answer: (d)

   All the other options are examples of loss of availability, while (d) is an example of loss of integrity.

10. Answer: (c)

   Threats (both privacy and security ones) might be much more severe when personal data processing activities are carried out online (either partially or fully) which is the case for options (a), (b), and (d). The correct answer is (c) as the data collection and processing are carried out offline (the individual has subscribed when attending a monthly gathering, and the monthly newsletter is sent to them via post.

11. Answer: (b)

   (a) is incorrect, because if roles and responsibilities are not clearly defined within an organisation, access and processing of personal data may be unauthorised which can be problematic. (c) is incorrect, because allowing employees to freely use their personal devices within an organisation could increase the risk of data leakage or unauthorised access. (d) is incorrect, because proper monitoring and logging measures can help an organisation prevent threats such as (un)intentional abuse of resources and personal data.

12. Answer: (d)

   Monitoring is a key element for every organisation to handle and control their privacy management activities and operations. In fact, a proper privacy programme should be continuously monitored, so that issues could be fixed in a timely manner, avoiding negative consequences such as compliance issues.

13. Answer: (a)

   An efficient monitoring mechanism in place can help an organisation comply with relevant legal privacy frameworks which in turn can lead to improved compliance simply because monitoring can ensure privacy goals and objectives are achieved and privacy-related issues are found and fixed in a timely manner.

14. Answer: (c)

   It is not acceptable to assess the intention of the individual, and the individual does not need to provide a reason for their request (options (a) and (b) are incorrect). As a result, your organisation needs to comply with the request, unless you find an individual's access request manifestly unfounded or excessive in nature. (d) is incorrect, because by default, an access request submitted by a dismissed employee, does not trigger the requirements of a manifestly unfounded or excessive request (e.g., repetitive access requests may be considered as an example of manifestly unfounded or excessive requests).

15. Answer: (c)

The data access right exercised by Ms. Garcia does not fulfil minimum privacy requirements, as her request concerns someone else's personal data (the employee who was occupying Ms. Garcia's parking lot) and not herself. Hence, the organisation shall refuse the request.

16. Answer: (d)

The university has already made it very clear in its privacy notice available on its website that individuals would need to submit any privacy-related queries or concerns in relation to the processing of their personal data to DPO@U.ORG. As a result, the safety staff are not involved in handling matters concerning the exercise of the privacy rights of individuals. Although the e-mail address of the safety staff was available on the premises of the university, the individual (Peter) cannot reasonably expect that this was an appropriate contact address for such requests, since the privacy notice clearly informed about the communication channel to be used for the exercise of individuals' privacy rights. Therefore, the university is not required to fulfil Peter's request as it is not sent to the correct contact point for the matters related to the processing of individuals's personal data.

17. Answer: (b)

There are some aspects that should be taken into account when deciding on the risk assessment and mitigation measures regarding incidents. Company ABC should assess the risks of this incident by taking into account the nature, sensitivity, volume, and context of personal data affected. In this scenario, no sensitive personal data is affected, and the number of affected individuals is not significant. Moreover, the ransomware encrypted personal data without exfiltrating it. Therefore, it seems that the confidentiality of personal data is not compromised and the risk to the fundamental rights and freedoms of individuals results from the lack of access to encrypted personal data. Furthermore, the company does not have a backup in electronic format which indicates that the data may be lost and the severity would depend on the impact on affected individuals. Considering the fact that it took 3 days for the company to restore the data and its potential impact on customers, a notification to the respective supervisory authority may be required. Notification to affected individuals may not be needed as it appears from the scenario that the incident was not likely to result in high risks to the fundamental rights and freedoms of individuals (the risk exists, but it is not high).

18. Answer: (a)

Organisations shall document any personal data breaches regardless of their risk level. This will help them demonstrate compliance when requested by a regulatory body.

19. Answer: (c)

    Except (c), all the other options are good examples of organisational
    and technical measures for preventing/mitigating the impact of internal
    human risk sources. It is good practice to disable open cloud services
    as remote connections to the servers of these services may result in
    potential data breaches such as unauthorised access.

20. Answer: (a)

    In this scenario, the billing information of an individual was wrongly
    sent to another individual. Considering that the billing information
    is related to an insurance plan, it may contain personal data such
    as the individual's name, address, physical and mental health status,
    lifestyle, etc. In addition, it appears that the identity validation
    measure of the insurance company can be easily bypassed (someone
    was able to pretend to be the intended client), and therefore, there
    is no guarantee if this vulnerability would not be exploited again.
    Hence, notification to both the competent supervisory authority and
    the affected individual seems to be reasonable.

21. Answer: (d)

    (a) is incorrect, because data is provided from a controller (Swedish
    insurance company) to a processor in a third country. Therefore,
    the provision of Chapter V will apply. (b) is incorrect, because the
    processing activities carried out by the processor (in the EU) is subject
    to the GDPR. The retailer is the controller which is established in a

third country, and therefore, any data disclosure from the processor in the EU to the controller in the third country is subject to Chapter V. (c) is incorrect, because the processing carried out by the Austrian bank and its processor (cloud service provider) is carried out in the context of their establishments in the EU and is therefore subject to the GDPR pursuant to its Article 3(1). However, the processing carried out by the sub-processor in Vietnam is to be considered as the passing of data from the EU processor (cloud service provider) to a sub-processor established in a third country (Vietnam). Therefore, Chapter V of the GDPR applies. As for option (d), it is worth mentioning, that although the individual has disclosed their personal data to a Brazilian online jewellery website, this does not constitute a transfer of personal data under Chapter V, since the data is not transferred by an exporter (either a controller or a processor), rather directly upon the individual's discretion.

22. Answer: (d)

(a), (b), and (c) are incorrect, because according to Article 46 (2) of the GDPR, all these options can be used as a tool for data transfers. Note that modernised Standard Contractual Clauses (SCCs) should be differentiated from old SCCs. On 4 June 2021, the European Commission issued modernised SCCs for data transfers from controllers/processors in the EU/EEA (or otherwise subject to the GDPR) to controllers/processors established outside the EU/EEA (and not subject to the GDPR) that replace the three sets of SCCs that were adopted under the previous Data Protection Directive 95/46. Since 27 September

2021, it is no longer possible to conclude contracts incorporating these old sets of SCCs. This is to be reconsidered though after the European Commission starts the process to adopt adequacy decision for the new EU-US Data Privacy Framework (which was jointly announced by the European Commission and the US in March 2022 and signed by the US president as an Executive Order in October 2022).

23. Answer: (a)

    (b) is incorrect, because it refers to another foundational principle of privacy-by-design which is *End-to-End Security* which ensures data is securely collected, processed, stored, and finally destroyed. (c) is incorrect, because it refers to principle *Proactive not Reactive; Preventative not Remedial* that indicates privacy-intrusive events should be anticipated and prevented before happening. (d) is incorrect, because it refers to principle *Respect for User Privacy* that demands user-centred and user-friendly settings, options, and interfaces. In fact, it indicates that the interests of individuals should be kept uppermost.

24. Answer: (c)

    Trustworthiness itself means worthy of being trusted to fulfil critical requirements. Trustworthiness of a system means the system meets critical requirements to be trusted. From a privacy perspective, a trustworthy system means a system that meets specific privacy requirements in addition to meeting other critical requirements.

25. Answer: (b)

    The organisation shall seek the advice of the DPO (where designated), when carrying out a DPIA.

26. Answer: (b)

According to Article 35 (1) of the GDPR, "where a type of processing, in particular, using new technologies, and taking into account the nature, scope, context and purposes of the processing, is likely to result in a high risk to the rights and freedoms of natural persons, the controller shall, prior to the processing, carry out an assessment of the impact of the envisaged processing operations on the protection of personal data". This is why (d) is incorrect. (a) and (c) are incorrect as well, because according to Article 35 (3)(a) and (c), these two scenarios would require a DPIA. (b) is correct as small-scale processing of sensitive data would not require a DPIA, e.g., the data processing activities of a local community doctor is not considered as a large-scale processing of sensitive data, and thus, does not trigger the requirement of a DPIA. This is also further clarified in Recital 91 of the GDPR, i.e., "the processing of personal data should not be considered to be on a large scale if the processing concerns personal data from patients or clients by an individual physician, other health care professional or lawyer. In such cases, a data protection impact assessment should not be mandatory".

27. Answer: (c)

In determining whether or not a DPIA is required, one would need to decide on whether data processing is likely to result in high risks. The geographical location of data processing does not trigger such a requirement. However, the geographical extent (e.g., a data processing which is carried out across 10 countries) is indeed influential.

28. Answer: (a)

   (b) is incorrect, because such a processing is aimed at systematically evaluating and monitoring individuals based on automated decision-making procedures which may have significant consequences on people's lives (Dutch scandal over families wrongly accused of benefit fraud is a good example of this). (c) is incorrect, because it involves systematic monitoring on a large scale. (d) is incorrect, because it is not only involving systematic monitoring of employees' private space (their home), but also innovative use of new technological and organisational solutions (metaverse). (a) is correct, because data processing activities of a lawyer is not considered as a large-scale processing of personal data, and thus, does not trigger the requirement of a DPIA.

29. Answer: (d)

   SFF is accountable for ensuring that the DPIA is carried out. To put this in a GDPR-context, SFF acts as the controller and the cloud service provider as the processor. Although the processor shall support/help the controller in conducting the DPIA, the controller is held responsible for ensuring that the DPIA is carried out.

30. Answer: (c)

   The assessment of the transparency of the processing is not necessary for a DPIA.

31. Answer: (a)

   The existing legal frameworks do not limit organisations in terms of choosing certain DPIA methodologies. In fact, it is up to an organisation to choose a methodology. However, it is widely recommended to use sector-specific DPIA methodologies as they enable an organisation to draw on specific sectorial knowledge by addressing certain aspects of a data processing activity such as specific types of processing procedures, threats, and risk likelihood.

32. Answer: (b)

There are no obligations for an organisation to publish a DPIA. There is also no obligation to communicate a DPIA to a competent supervisory authority (unless in case of a prior consultation when the outcome of the DPIA indicates high risks and risks cannot be mitigated despite the fact that risk mitigation measures are in place by the organisation or if requested by a competent supervisory authority). In other words, it is good practice to publish some aspects of the DPIA such as a summary or an outcome of the DPIA. This is also well-aligned with the principle of transparency that may ultimately increase individuals' and stakeholders' trust.

33. Answer: (b)

(a) is incorrect, because it is indeed well-aligned with the principle of storage limitation. (c) is incorrect, because it is in line with the principle of transparency and accountability. (d) is incorrect, because it is in line with the principle of purpose limitation. (b) is correct, because implementing preferences for automated processes in the app, which when enabled, would make it impossible to gain knowledge of processed data, thus, being in line with the principle of data minimisation.

34. Answer: (c)

The raw data obtained for this research could only be published if minimal security precautions would be in place, such as anonymising the data. The publication of the dataset could potentially expose individuals (Twitter account holders) to the risk of discrimination or discredit because of the non-anonymised political profiling. This is due to the fact, that the dataset contained information about their political opinions of the individuals whose accounts were analysed. To learn more about this real case, read the decision made by the Belgian Data Protection Authority about *"political profiling of Internet users who tweeted about the Benalla affair"*.

35. Answer: (a)

Options (b), (c), and (d) all point to an *organisational* structure for managing data protection and information governance such as clear policies and responsibilities and effective information flows. However, (a) is clearly pointing to the *operational* aspects of practical implementation of data protection and information governance which demands appropriate and adequate authority, support, and resources for data protection and information governance staff to carry out their responsibilities effectively.

36. Answer: (d)

Options (a), (b), and (c) are all essential features of appropriate policies and procedures in relation to privacy and governance within an organisation. (d) is incorrect, because an organisation shall make sure to review and potentially update policies and procedures without undue delay when they require changes, e.g., because of operational changes, court or regulatory decisions or changes in regulatory guidance. Therefore, reviewing policies and procedures at fixed intervals does not seem to be a good idea due to the ever-evolving nature of the privacy and data governance landscape.

37. Answer: (c)

    (a) is incorrect, because in an efficient privacy training programme, the training needs of all staff should be considered (no prioritisation of certain groups over others) as equally important (although this does not rule out the importance of implementing more intense training for staff working at the front line of privacy-related affairs). (b) is incorrect, because a privacy training programme shall not only focus on national-level requirements, rather national-, international-, and sectoral-specific requirements. (d) is incorrect, because depending on the responsibilities of staff, specialised roles or functions with key privacy responsibilities (e.g., DPO) shall receive additional training beyond the basic level provided to all staff.

38. Answer: (c)

    Within an organisation, a privacy policy is an internal document aimed at communicating to staff and whoever is going to use and process personal data. A privacy policy in fact deals with broader aspects of privacy and data protection in an organisation. By contrast, a privacy notice is an external document aimed at communicating to customers or users of an organisation.

39. Answer: (c)

Any organisation shall frequently conduct comprehensive data mapping exercises to build up a picture of what personal data is held and where. This is also often referred to as information audits to find out what personal data is held and to understand how the information flows through an organisation. It is important to make sure that the data map is always up to date.

40. Answer: (b)

Such details are not needed to be included in ROPA.

41. Answer: (b)

A validly obtained consent requires a positive opt-in (not opt-out). For instance, the use of pre-ticked boxes is not deemed to be a valid way of obtaining consent. (a) is incorrect, because consent requests should indeed be kept separate from other terms and conditions. When a consent request is tied to the performance of a contract, it means an individual who does not wish to make their personal data available for processing by an organisation, would not be able to benefit from the services they had wished for. (c) is incorrect, because specific consent requests can be deemed as good practice. (d) is incorrect, because for consent to be informed individuals should be aware at least of the identity of the organisation and the purposes of the processing for which the personal data is collected.

42. Answer: (d)

For a privacy training programme to be effective, staff must be actively engaged in privacy training. They need to be educated in privacy and data protection generally, and those who deal with personal data directly, need additional training tailored to their roles. Importantly, training and education need to be recurrent, and the content of the programme needs to be periodically revisited and updated. For privacy training and education to be effective, it must be mandatory for all employees before they access personal data and periodically thereafter.

43. Answer: (a)

This is indeed a complex scenario. Obviously, the bar has collected the data lawfully as clear signage was in place to inform individuals of their biometric data being captured on the bar's premises. Therefore, option (d) is incorrect. When it comes to Company ABC, things get a little bit more complex. In this scenario, it is important to examine whether there is a legal basis for Company ABC to obtain the CCTV footage. For this scenario, *legitimate interest* might be a lawful processing ground. When relying on legitimate interest, three main conditions must be met by the organisation:

1. There must be the existence of a legitimate interest justifying the processing;

2. the processing of the personal data must be necessary for the realisation of the legitimate interest; and

3. that interest must prevail over the rights and interests of individuals.

As it is obvious from the scenario, there has been an allegation of a serious assault committed by Employee A against Employee B and the bar has provided a copy of the CCTV footage to Employee A's employer (Company ABC, which is also the employer of Employee B) so that the employer could properly investigate that incident and the allegations made. As the incident had occurred during the employer's social event, the employer might have been liable for any injuries to any employee that could have occurred during the incident. Accordingly, the CCTV was processed in furtherance of the employer organisation's obligation to protect the health and safety of its employees. As the protection of health and safety of employees is a legitimate interest, it can be argued that Company ABC's reliance on legitimate interest is justifiable (condition #1 is met). Thus, the disclosure of the CCTV footage in this instance was necessary for the legitimate interests pursued by Company ABC, so that it could investigate and validate the incident (condition #2 is met). This was also previously reflected in a judgment of the Court of Justice of the European Union (CJEU) in the Riga regional security police case (case number: C-13/16) which highlighted the fact that it is important to take into account that data protection is not utilised in an obstructive fashion where a limited amount of personal data is concerned. Having said that, it would have been unreasonable to expect the bar to refuse a request by Company ABC to view and take a copy of the CCTV footage, against a backdrop of allegations of a serious assault on its premises, especially where the personal data had been limited to the incident in question and had not otherwise been disclosed. As for the third condition (balancing the interest of Company ABC against Employee A's rights and interests), it is important to note that a refusal of the request made by Company ABC to view the CCTV footage might have impeded the full investigation of an alleged serious assault, and Company ABC's ability to protect the health and welfare of its employees. Therefore, it can be argued that it was reasonable, justifiable and necessary for the bar to process the CCTV footage by providing it to Company ABC, and that the legitimate interest of Company ABC took precedence over the rights and freedoms of Employee A (condition #3 is met).

44. Answer: (d)

Neither the bar nor Company ABC's needs to obtain Employee A's consent as the bar has made it transparent that CCTVs are operating on its premises. Also, obtaining consent from Employee A by Company ABC is not relevant as the data collector was the bar who had a valid reason to operate CCTV on its premises. Therefore, options (a) and (b) are incorrect. (c) is incorrect as well, because no legal obligation exists for the bar to disclose the footage.

45. Answer: (c)

A significant portion of data breaches occur due to unauthorised disclosure of personal data being sent in error to a wrong address. In such circumstances, it is highly critical to act quickly. If possible, the e-mail shall be recalled as soon as possible, and if not possible, the organisation shall contact the unintended recipient and ask them to delete it and confirm they have done so.

46. Answer: (a)

The hospital has contracted a healthcare agency to provide staff to work in the hospital (nurses). Hence, it is the hospital's responsibility to do due diligence and make sure any contractors/processors they engage in data processing activities are fully trained and prepared to comply with privacy and data protection requirements.

47. Answer: (b)

Privacy laws do not prevent or prohibit the use of a sign language interpreter or similar services where a person who is deaf or hard of hearing needs to use these services when engaging with a service provider. In fact, service providers are obliged to implement appropriate organisational and technical security measures to protect the integrity and confidentiality of clients' personal data. Importantly, these measures must not disproportionately disadvantage those who need to use a sign language interpreter or a form of text service. Hence, (b) is correct, because privacy laws shall not be used as a barrier by a service provider to prevent access to services and to discriminate against people on the basis of their disability.

48. Answer: (c)

In the context of the GDPR, certification under Articles 42 and 43 is an accountability tool "for the purpose of demonstrating compliance with the GDPR of processing operations by controllers and processors". Options (a), (b), and (d) are all deemed to be fulfilled by approved certification mechanisms as referred to in Article 42. For further details, see Articles 24 (3), 25 (3), and 32 (3).

49. Answer: (b)

For an organisation to implement the defined privacy strategy, it needs to structure a privacy team. Privacy governance models are mechanisms that enable an organisation to achieve this goal.

50. Answer: (b)

The idea of an employee privacy policy within an organisation is for the organisation to provide a very clear overview of the overarching procedures, policies, and measures that are in place to specify the organisation's rules and procedures for gathering, using and disclosing personal data. For instance, an organisation might want its employee to only use certain so-called approved tools and software on its premises. Hence, this document is addressed to employees, and thus, the employees' statement is not of relevance.

51. Answer: (a)

Organisations shall frequently conduct comprehensive data mapping exercises to build up a picture of what personal data is held and where. This is also sometimes referred to as information audits to find out what personal data is held and to understand how the information flows through an organisation. Having an efficient data mapping strategy can help an organisation develop appropriate data retention and destruction policies to ensure personal data is only kept as long as required for the lawful purposes pursued by the organisation.

52. Answer: (c)

(a) is incorrect, because although the mobile app is providing an opt-out option for the voice assistant functionality, this functionality is already enabled (unless the individual objects). (b) is incorrect, because pre-ticked opt-in cookie settings are not aligned with best privacy-by-default practices (if the user decides not to opt-in, then they have to make the effort to uncheck pre-ticked opt-in settings). (c) is correct because the browser disables trackers by default (upon the first time the user uses it). As a result, no further action or effort is needed from the user as their privacy is respected by default. (d) is incorrect, because the 'Do Not Track Me' indicates that individuals are tracked by default. Thus, individuals need to enable this option to ensure they are not tracked any longer.

53. Answer: (a)

    In this scenario, the news media company may not be obliged to delete this information from its website as this is against the right to freedom of expression and information, including processing for journalistic purposes. However, the individual could lodge a complaint with respective search engines and ask them to un-index this information from their search results as the search engines are acting as the data controller in relation to processing activities related to search indexes.

54. Answer: (d)

    According to best practices, an organisation shall try to use multiple alternative (and not single) channels for communicating their data processing practices to individuals. QR codes and layered interfaces are an example of such communication channels. Except (d), all other options are examples of good approaches towards a fair and transparent data processing notice.

55. Answer: (d)

Privacy laws across the globe set a higher expectation in relation to data protection requirements when it comes to children. Whilst the other age categories are of great importance when it comes to compliance matters, children under 13 years are always considered as the most vulnerable group because they may be less aware of the risks involved. Thus, compliance with data protection principles and in particular fairness should be central to an organisation's activities and operations in relation to children's personal data processing.

56. Answer: (b)

Your organisation shall make sure that your consent request is concise, separate from other terms and conditions, and easy to understand. Pre-ticked opt-in boxes shall be avoided as well.

57. Answer: (a)

Individuals shall have the right to obtain from organisations confirmation as to whether or not personal data concerning them is being processed, and, where that is the case, access to the personal data and some other information such as the purposes of the processing and categories of personal data concerned. Under some circumstances, privacy laws (such as the GDPR) allow organisations to charge individuals for data access requests, e.g., where the individuals request further copies of their personal data, the organisation may charge a reasonable fee based on administrative costs.

58. Answer: (c)

There has been a significant growth in data collection and proliferation over the last decade by organisations. As a result, organisations need to pay extra attention to their data governance and management policies. Handling a data access request requires the implementation of data governance policies to ensure an organisation would respond to such requests appropriately (and timely) and can defend itself if brought before regulators. Establishing a decentralised process to handle these requests is not good practice. This is mainly because upon receiving a request from an individual, cooperation among different units, teams, or departments might be needed to handle the request. This gets even more critical as organisations shall typically provide a response to these requests within a certain time frame. As such, having a centralised policy at hand can help process these requests more efficiently.

59. Answer: (a)

Privacy education and awareness programmes can help an organisation to increase the awareness of staff about the way that organisation handles, manages, operates, and protects privacy, including the special role that staff play. For a privacy education and awareness programme to be effective, it is important to make sure that the programme is attractive and engaging enough as the world of information privacy and security might be complex per se. Additionally, a reinforced privacy awareness and education programme means that the programme is not supposed to serve as a once-in-a-lifetime experience. It means that the education and awareness campaigns shall be iterative to make sure staff are kept up-to-date in relation to the latest technological, legal, governance, and business developments.

60. Answer: (b)

Organisations shall make sure their policies in relation to privacy education and awareness programmes are flexible. Policies stability may result in an organisation not being able to accommodate fast-growing requirements in relation to its privacy, security, compliance and governance needs. This is why (b) is correct. (a) is incorrect, as efficient communications are indeed a key factor in the success of a privacy awareness and education programme. (c) and (d) are incorrect, because both internal and external education and awareness play an important role in the success of a privacy programme. Internal programmes refer to an organisation's education and awareness policies aiming at educating and increasing the awareness of its staff, including different teams, units, departments, and stakeholders within the organisation. External programmes, on the other hand, refer to an organisation's education and awareness policies aiming at educating and increasing the awareness of its customers by building their trust and confidence through highlighting the organisation's commitment to fulfilling privacy, security, and compliance requirements.

61. Answer: (d)

Although efficient privacy education and awareness training may reduce potential privacy, security, and compliance risks, it is not supposed to be deemed as a profit-generating matter. In fact, organising privacy education and awareness training may be costly for an organisation (in terms of resources, staff needed, types of equipment, etc.). Thus, other options, i.e., (a), (b), and (c) are more realistic to be used as metrics for evaluating privacy education and awareness training.

62. Answer: (b)

Privacy engineering is the most likely match for this definition as its ultimate goal is to bridge the gap between legal and compliance requirements and the technical implementation of these requirements from an engineering perspective. Privacy- and security-by-design are both facilitators for privacy engineering. As for privacy-enhancing technologies, these are technologies implemented and deployed through a privacy engineering concept to fulfil different privacy and data protection principles such as anonymisation.

63. Answer: (c)

(a) is incorrect, because information security controls that prevent an incident from happening are *preventative controls*. (b) is incorrect, because information security controls that discover/identify an incident are *detective controls*. (d) is incorrect, because it is the responsibility of *access controls* to restrict access to data files. *Corrective controls* can help an organisation to confine damages resulting from an incident and recover to a normal setting as soon and effectively as possible after an incident.

64. Answer: (c)

Whilst information privacy and information security are different, they overlap a lot. Confidentiality, integrity, and availability are all information security requirements that are different from information privacy requirements such as accuracy and data minimisation. However, this difference does not mean that they are decoupled.

65. Answer: (b)

(a) is incorrect, because the principle of least privilege or least privilege control is used to allow the least privilege access needed to complete a task. (c) is incorrect, because segregation/separation of duties is a basic internal control that prevents or detects errors and irregularities to ensure no individuals are in a position to access information that they should not. (d) is incorrect, because remote access service refers to any combination of hardware and software to enable remote access to tools or information that typically resides on a network of IT devices within an organisation.

66. Answer: (d)

(a) is incorrect, because the problem escalation procedure refers to the process of escalating a problem up from junior to senior staff, and ultimately to higher levels of management. (b) is incorrect, because security testing refers to ensuring that the modified or new system includes appropriate controls and does not introduce any security holes that might compromise other systems or misuse information. (c) is incorrect, because performance management is the ability to manage any type of measurement, including employees, teams, processes, operational or financial measurements. User access management refers to all activities that help an organisation encapsulate people, processes and services to identify and manage the data used in an information system to authenticate users and grant or deny access rights to data and system resources. A clean desk policy ensures that important (and confidential) letters, files, and documents are removed from a desk and locked away when the items are not in use or an employee leaves their workstation which can ultimately reduce the risk of information theft, fraud, or a privacy/security breach caused by sensitive information being left unattended and visible.

67. Answer: (a)

An incident often refers to something bad happening at an organisation. However, it does not always mean that a data breach has occurred. For instance, an organisation suffering from a denial of service attack is experiencing an incident as no breach has occurred. But if any exfiltration would occur, then this might be deemed as a data breach. However, note that a breach might be even broader than exfiltration of personal data. For instance, under the EU GDPR a "personal data breach means a breach of security leading to the accidental or unlawful destruction, loss, alteration, unauthorised disclosure of, or access to, personal data transmitted, stored or otherwise processed". Therefore, exfiltration or data leakage is not the only consideration that should be made when determining if a personal data breach has occurred. Another example is when an organisation fails to have timely access to the personal data (e.g., due to a ransomware attack encrypting data). This can be considered as a personal data breach because the organisation has lost access to personal data.

68. Answer: (d)

(a) is incorrect, because business continuity plans (BCPs) support an organisation to specify how their business will continue operating during an unplanned disruption in service. Since incidents might cause unplanned disruption in services, it is highly crucial to integrate incident response plans with BCPs. (b) is incorrect, because measures to escalate suspicious activities and incidents are key players in an incident response plan as they specify how to hand off the task to more experienced or specialised teams or units, including who should be notified when an incident occurs, who an incident should be escalated to if the first responder is not available, etc. (c) is incorrect, because communication with different stakeholder (e.g., vendors, competent supervisory authorities, and affected individuals) is important as well. (d) is correct, because it is not efficient to treat each incident as a crisis. Organisations shall seek policies that determine the organisation's risk level upon suffering from an incident to react accordingly.

69. Answer: (d)

    Statement A is incorrect, because there is no need to propagate information regarding how an incident is being dealt with to all staff. In fact, incident response teams shall make sure adequate information is communicated to relevant teams. In other words, only communicate the required amount of information to the required number of recipients/stakeholders. This does not mean that internal announcements should be avoided. Internal announcements are vital not only for the sake of transparency but also integrity and credibility. Staff shall be appropriately informed and briefed about the incident. Guidelines could also be supplied to ensure risks are minimised. Statement B is incorrect as well, because it is not good practice to give the incident response team the autonomy to confirm legal requirements. The legal team shall always be involved in such matters.

70. Answer: (c)

Trend analysis is a well-established practice of collecting information and attempting to spot a pattern. In the context of metrics of a privacy programme, it refers to identifying patterns when analysing the programme. For instance, a descending trend observed in the total number of incidents that occurred at an organisation might be identified using this technique.

71. Answer: (a)

Patience is a key element for organisations to be compliant with privacy and data protection laws. In fact, compliance is a journey and progress which is strengthened along the way. This is why Statement A is correct. Statement B is incorrect, as not every organisation needs to be at the maximum acceptable level of security to be deemed as an organisation with a mature privacy programme. This is indeed stipulated by the American Institute of Certified Public Accountants (AICPA) and the Canadian Institute of Chartered Accountants (CICA) Privacy Maturity Model where "it was also recognised that, based on an organisation's approach to risk, not all privacy initiatives would need to reach the highest level on the maturity model".

72. Answer: (a)

Generally Accepted Privacy Principles (GAPP) have been developed by the AICPA and CICA "from a business perspective, referencing some, but by no means all, significant local, national, and international privacy regulations. GAPP operationalises complex privacy requirements into a single privacy objective that is supported by 10 privacy principles". These principles are as follows: (1) Management; (2) notice; (3) choice and consent; (4) collection; (5) use, retention and disposal; (6) access; (7) disclosure to third parties; (8) security for privacy; (9) quality; and (10) monitoring and enforcement.

73. Answer: (a)

In order to reach a certain level of maturity (e.g., the fifth one), an organisation has to make sure all the requirements for previous levels (1, 2, 3, and 4) are met.

74. Answer: (b)

Statement A is incorrect, because depending on an organisation's approach to risk, not all privacy strategies and initiatives would need to reach the highest level on the maturity model. Statement B is correct, because under the PMM, it might be the case that an organisation's personal information privacy practices would be at various levels. This is highly dependent on legislative requirements, business needs and corporate policies or the status of the organisation's privacy initiatives. For instance, in terms of the first GAPP principle (management), company's privacy policies (the first sub-principle for management principle is 'privacy policies') may reach the *optimised* level on the PMM, meaning that management monitors compliance with policies and procedures concerning personal information. Non-compliance issues are efficiently detected and appropriate measures are in place to ensure compliance. Nevertheless, the same company might reach the *ad hoc* level on the PMM for the seventh principle (disclosure to third parties).

75. Answer: (d)

To calculate the overall maturity level, an organisation is not supposed to stick to a pre-defined formula. In fact, it is up to the organisation to decide if a simple mathematical average would suffice. If not, the organisation could simply determine weightings to be given to various criteria depending on the organisation's policies and requirements. This is why options (a), (b), and (c) are incorrect, because it is not 'always' the case that an organisation shall follow different or same weighting or even a simple mathematical average. In case the organisation would decide to assign different weightings, the organisation shall document the rationale behind such weighting, so that it would be possible to re-construct or use the same weighting for future references and benchmarking. This is why (d) is correct.

76. Answer: (c)

The PMM encompasses five maturity levels as follows:

1 Ad hoc: At this level, almost no standards exist. This level is called ad hoc simply because procedures are generally applied in an ad hoc manner. They are informal, incomplete, and inconsistently applied.

2 Repeatable: At this level, some standardisation of procedures exist, although most processes are still immature (e.g., they are not well-documented and do not cover relevant requirements).

3 Defined: This level is a significant step for the organisation as procedures and processes are regularly and effectively documented and implemented.

4 Managed: This level marks the advance of the organisation in its use of privacy management programme. At this level, essential reviews are in place to examine the effectiveness of implemented controls.

5 Optimised: This level is distinguished from the previous one (managed) as it is very much organisationally rigorous and process-disciplined. At this level, regular reviews and feedback are used to ensure the organisation proactively uses optimisation techniques.

77. Answer: (b)

(a) is incorrect, as implementing monitoring measures and processes for ensuring privacy in relation to information being exchanged across HR units is critical. (c) is incorrect, because data breach monitoring can be deemed as a monitoring measure to figure out if an organisation's privacy programme (e.g., privacy education and awareness training) is implemented appropriately and aligned with regulatory requirements. (d) is incorrect, because many organisation are nowadays outsourcing their operations to third party vendors and suppliers. Therefore, it is important to make sure (monitor) these vendors and suppliers to comply with privacy compliance and data protection requirements.

78. Answer: (a)

Whilst the data processing resulting from the access control mechanism might be justifiable under the legitimate interest ground (to comply with legal obligations concerning unauthorised access to the server room), it is not well-justified to rely on such an intrusive data processing operation to evaluate the performance of employees. In fact, the continuous monitoring of the frequency and exact entrance and exit times of the employees cannot be justified if this data is also used for another purpose, such as employee performance evaluation.

79. Answer: (d)

When it comes to consent, an organisation has to demonstrate that individuals have given consent to the processing operation. The majority of data protection regimes state that consent requests should be provided in an intelligible and easily accessible form, using clear and plain language that should not contain unfair terms. Hence, consent should be informed, specific, freely given, and unambiguous. Importantly, consent should not be regarded as freely given if an individual has no genuine or free choice or is unable to refuse or withdraw consent without detriment which is the case in this scenario (if a user would decide to withdraw consent at a later point, the dating app would only work to a limited extent which can be deemed as a detriment). Therefore, consent obtained in this way would be invalid, and thus, any data processing would be unlawful.

80. Answer: (a)

The organisation's direct telephone marketing calls using an automated calling system is an example of unsolicited telephone advertising (Statement A is correct) as the organisation has not obtained consent validly. For direct telephone marketing calls using an automated calling system consent is often needed (Statement B is incorrect). Although the organisation has obtained individuals' consent for directing marketing purposes, it is obtained on an invalid basis as the organisation has merged consent with the provisions of the contract.

81. Answer: (a)

For direct telephone marketing calls using an automated calling system consent is needed. Although the organisation has obtained the individuals' consent for directing marketing purposes, the consent is invalid as it is with the provisions of the contract, i.e., if the consent to direct marketing was not given, an individual could not subscribe. Therefore, consent and the way it is obtained is invalid (Statement A is correct). Hence, the consent was not specifically requested for direct marketing and together with the subscription and contract terms, it did not constitute voluntary consent for the purpose of direct marketing (Statement B is incorrect).

82. Answer: (c)

The CCPA requires companies to enable customers to opt-out of the sale of their personal data. Note that under the California Privacy Rights Act (CPRA), this has expanded to include opt-out of sharing.

83. Answer: (a)

This is an example of on-demand privacy notices where users are given the option to read privacy policy notices at their own discretion and whenever they demand it.

84. Answer: (b)

Although it is true that some departments/units/roles within an organisation are more involved in the successful execution and delivery of a privacy programme, it is the ultimate responsibility of each individual working at an organisation to follow information privacy and security requirements and controls. A nicely designed privacy programme might fall apart if an individual would not commit to the organisation's information privacy and security measures and controls.

85. Answer: (d)

Corrective controls can help an organisation confine damages resulting from an incident and recover to a normal setting as soon as possible after an incident.

86. Answer: (b)

This is indeed an example of an organisation that considers policies and procedures across the organisation with privacy and data protection in mind which is the ultimate goal of privacy-by-design.

87. Answer: (b)

The idea behind a ransomware attack is to prevent access to computers, data, and resources. A successful ransomware attack can severely affect the availability of services and operations across an organisation.

88. Answer: (a)

All relevant decisions concerning a DPIA should always be documented, even in those cases where the initial analysis of a proposed personal data processing activity indicates no need for a DPIA. This will help an organisation to better demonstrate compliance.

89. Answer: (b)

Generally, there are three main encryption concepts known as encryption in-transit (protecting data when being transferred over a network such as the internet), in-use (protecting data when in-use, e.g., by another entity than the organisation itself), and at-rest (protecting data when stored on a disk). Given this scenario, the attackers have been able to decrypt the stored encrypted data on the organisation's storage which indicates that the organisation has failed to safeguard health data at-rest.

90. Answer: (a)

One should distinguish the term *data governance* from *information governance*. Data governance is a subset of information governance and primarily deals with technical aspects of data processing such as data security, data quality, data storage capabilities and anything related to structured data. Information governance, on the other hand, deals with the organisational aspects of data processing such as risk management, compliance, policies which also involves people (e.g., employees) and mainly focuses on managing procedures related to information (unstructured data).

CHAPTER 4

Answers for Practice Exam II

Answer Key for Practice Exam II

Q	A	Q	A	Q	A	Q	A	Q	A
1	c	19	d	37	a	55	a	73	c
2	d	20	d	38	c	56	c	74	c
3	d	21	c	39	b	57	b	75	c
4	b	22	b	40	a	58	b	76	d
5	b	23	a	41	c	59	b	77	c
6	c	24	d	42	d	60	d	78	a
7	b	25	b	43	a	61	c	79	b
8	d	26	b	44	a	62	a	80	d
9	a	27	b	45	d	63	a	81	c
10	a	28	c	46	b	64	c	82	c
11	c	29	c	47	c	65	a	83	b
12	b	30	c	48	c	66	c	84	d
13	a	31	a	49	a	67	d	85	d
14	a	32	d	50	b	68	b	86	a
15	d	33	d	51	a	69	c	87	c
16	b	34	b	52	a	70	c	88	c
17	a	35	c	53	d	71	c	89	b
18	d	36	a	54	d	72	b	90	d

Detailed Answers for Practice Exam II

1. Answer: (c)

   A DPIA mainly deals with risks to individuals and how well an organisation is prepared to mitigate or at least minimise the impact of such risks. Risks to the business is not of relevance when conducting a DPIA. The main purpose of a DPIA is to protect the fundamental rights (the right to privacy) of individuals, not businesses.

2. Answer: (d)

   Option (d) is the more likely first step that this organisation should take towards establishing an efficient privacy governance programme. In fact, defining business and compliance needs is the foundational building block of every privacy governance programme. For instance, depending on a compliance requirement (e.g., HIPPA or GDPR), an organisation may not be allowed to process personal data of certain individuals beyond a certain retention period that may ultimately affect the business needs of an organisation (e.g., establishing organisational procedures to stop personal data processing that may conflict with compliance requirements).

3. Answer: (d)

   (d) is correct, because it is vital for every organisation to make sure that the DPO does not receive any instructions regarding the exercise of their tasks. Moreover, organisations shall make sure the DPO's tasks and responsibilities do not result in a conflict of interests with their privacy-related tasks and duties.

4. Answer: (b)

This is an example of loss of confidentiality.

5. Answer: (b)

This is an example of loss of availability.

6. Answer: (c)

Except (c), all the other options are examples of risks associated with the BYOD policy.

7. Answer: (b)

Proactive not Reactive; Preventative not Remedial refers to the fact that privacy-intrusive events should be anticipated and prevented before they occur. (a) is incorrect, because it refers to another principle of privacy-by-design (*End-to-End Security*) which ensures data is securely collected, processed, stored, and destroyed. (c) is incorrect, because it refers to principle *Respect for User Privacy* that demands user-centred and user-friendly settings, options, and interfaces. In fact, it indicates that the interests of individuals should be kept uppermost. (d) is incorrect, because it refers to principle *Full Functionality* that seeks to implement both strong security and strong privacy.

8. Answer: (d)

Risk acceptance, risk transfer, risk mitigation, and risk avoidance are the four privacy risk treatments used when dealing with privacy risks.

9. Answer: (a)

An organisation's investment in planning and improving its incident management can help reduce incident time response and recovery actions which will ultimately help reduce potential impact (resulted from incidents) on day-to-day services and operations.

10. Answer: (a)

This is an example of ad hoc level in which procedures are often reactive, informal, incomplete, and inconsistently applied.

11. Answer: (c)

It may happen that organisations withdraw already implemented privacy and security controls. Examples of this are when the capability offered by the control is incorporated into another control, and thus, making an already implemented control redundant (options (a) and (b) are incorrect). A control may also be deemed as no longer necessary due to many reasons, e.g., deprecating a feature in a product that had been enabling users of an app to share personal data publicly. High implementation costs is not a good reason to justify the fact that a control needs to be withdrawn. If the implementation cost is too high, the organisation shall seek alternatives or simplified solutions to keep the implementation cost at a reasonable level.

12. Answer: (b)

Disabling expired or inactive accounts will support the implementation of principle of least privilege, reducing the risk of unauthorised individuals gaining access to a system.

13. Answer: (a)

Insufficient attention to trustworthiness of IT products and systems can adversely affect an organisation's capability to carry out its business functions. Trustworthiness of IT products and systems is often determined by two factors, namely functionality and assurance. A system that exhibits appropriate functionality and assurance is deemed to be more trustworthy.

14. Answer: (a)

Within an organisation, Acceptable Use Policy (AUP) is a set of guidelines and policies that mandate how staff can use devices, systems, and services which also includes stipulations around privileges, responsibilities and sanctions associated with such uses. Except (a), all the others are examples of objectives of AUPs.

15. Answer: (d)

Option (a) is an example of what you know. Option (b) is an example of what you have. Option (c) is an example of where you are.

16. Answer: (b)

Checking whether an individual is allowed to use transport facilities could be accommodated without comparing the personal data on the card's chip with a database. It would suffice, for instance, to have a special electronic image, such as a bar code upon being passed in front of the reading device, which would confirm whether the card is valid or not. Such a system would not record who used which transport facility at what time.

17. Answer: (a)

Except option (a), all other options are examples of preventative controls. Preventive controls aim at decreasing the likelihood of threats before they occur. Option (a) is a detective control where to goal is to detect a threat after it has occurred.

18. Answer: (d)

    Whilst all options are likely to intensify the severity of this attack, option (d) is more likely to do so. Lack of backup data could make it very difficult to restore normal operations swiftly after the attack. This is even more crucial when it comes to critical sectors such as energy suppliers where many people and their lives rely on them.

19. Answer: (d)

    Data exfiltration started after leaked credentials were exploited as far back as January 2018. This shows that an early incident detection and response could have played a key role in preventing this attack.

20. Answer: (d)

    This is the definition of integrity as one of the information security principles. Note that, manageability is a privacy engineering objective.

21. Answer: (c)

    Privacy requirements traceability allows an organisation to iteratively assess privacy controls for their effectiveness in meeting the privacy requirements and managing privacy risks. By creating traceability between privacy controls and privacy requirements, an organisation can better demonstrate accountability between its services and products which can ultimately result in meeting privacy goals.

22. Answer: (b)

    This is an example of role-based access control in which access to resources is granted depending on individuals' roles, e.g., HR department may not need access to confidential financial documents to perform their day-to-day job, whereas this is not the case for the vice president working in the finance department. Remember, rule-based and policy-based are the same and often used interchangeably.

23. Answer: (a)

Option (b) is an example of risk transfer where it is highly recommended to transfer or share the risk when an organisation is not able/ready to deal with it themselves. This could be done through contractual agreements or using an insurance provider. Options (c) and (d) are examples of risk mitigation where administrative or technical methods (in this case, hourly backups and encryption) are used to minimize risk until an acceptable risk tolerance level is reached. Option (a) is an example of risk avoidance as instead of asking users their exact birth of date to determine if they are above 18, the website asks a simple binary question to determine if a user is eligible to use the website which ultimately avoids potential future risks (such as interrogating users by requesting excessive information such as their exact date of birth for a basic reason of determining if they are eligible to use the website).

24. Answer: (d)

Authentication is about verifying the identity of users by confirming who they say they are, while authorisation is the process of establishing the rights and permissions the users have.

25. Answer: (b)

Except option (b), all other options are example of detective controls. Option (b) is a preventative control (e.g, passwords are a type of access controls).

26. Answer: (b)

A zero-day vulnerability is a software vulnerability discovered by attackers before an organisation becomes aware of it. As a result of organisations not being aware of such vulnerabilities, no patch exists to fix them which makes such attacks more successful. Using risk-based vulnerability management tools can help to prioritise patch assets depending on an organisation's needs and use-cases.

27. Answer: (b)

Role-Based access control is based on allowing users access to resources depending on their roles, whereas Policy-Based access control does the same depending on pre-defined rules and policies.

28. Answer: (c)

This is an example of attribute-based access control in which when users attempt to access resources (only access to PDF, JPG, and PNG files is allowed), policies enforce access decisions based on the attributes of the subject (employees in HR department), resource (files), action (read and write), and environment involved (server room).

29. Answer: (c)

Except option (c), all the others are benefits of privacy risks assessment.

30. Answer: (c)

NIST Privacy Framework suggests four main sources for deriving organisational-level privacy requirements, namely legal environment (e.g., privacy laws), organisational policies, relevant standards (e.g., ISO 27001), and privacy principles.

31. Answer: (a)

There are four types of responses to privacy risks. Mitigating the risk refers to applying technical and/or policy measures to minimise the risk. Transferring the risk refers to transferring risk to other entities (privacy notices are examples of transferring risk to users). Avoiding the risk refers to determining whether continuing the processing of personal data is going to result in risks and whether it would be beneficial to stop data processing to avoid those risks. Accepting the risk refers to determining whether potential risks are going to have no or minimum impacts on individuals, and therefore, it is not necessary to mitigate them.

32. Answer: (d)

When appointing a DPO for an organisation, it is of particular importance to make sure a DPO's tasks and responsibilities do not give rise to conflicts of an organisation's interests. In other words, the DPO cannot hold a position within an organisation that leads them to determine the purposes and the means of the processing of personal data. (a) is incorrect, because this is indeed the role of a Chief Information Officer (CIO) which directly conflicts with DPO's responsibilities. (b) is incorrect, because this is the role of a Chief Information Security Officer (CISO) which again conflicts with DPO's responsibilities. Similarly, (c) is incorrect, because this is the role of a Chief Legal Officer (or Head of Legal) which conflicts with DPO's responsibilities. (d) is correct, because this is indeed one of the most important tasks of a DPO (analysing and checking the compliance of processing activities).

33. Answer: (d)

One should distinguish the term *data governance* from *information governance*. Data governance is a subset of information governance and primarily deals with technical aspects of data processing such as data security, data quality, data storage capabilities and anything related to structured data. Information governance, on the other hand, deals with the organisational aspects of data processing such as risk management, compliance, policies which also involves people (e.g., employees) that mainly focuses on managing procedures related to information (unstructured data).

34. Answer: (b)

Requiring all employees to change their password does not seem to be a reasonable and proportionate effort and may not be necessary at all, depending on the nature of the breached data (option (a) is incorrect). Option (c) also seems to be irrelevant as an immediate action as the breach is not resulted from the use of personal devices within the organisation's networks, rather it has occurred on the vendor's side. Not all privacy breaches require a notification to a supervisory authority and this can only be determined after careful investigation of the breach itself, e.g., the nature, sensitivity, and scope of affected personal data and impacted individuals (option (d) is incorrect).

35. Answer: (c)

    The main objective of privacy-by-design is to minimise the collection, processing, and storing of personal data to a minimum required amount (if you do not need the data, do not collect it in the first place). Remember, privacy-by-default is a subset (one of the principles) of privacy-by-design.

36. Answer: (a)

    It is almost impossible to protect personal data without knowing what types of personal data an organisation has collected and where the data is located. Hence, creating data inventory policies and procedures can be deemed as the first step in protecting personal data as data inventories contain very useful information around different data types collected, processed, and stored within an organisation. This will help to have a clear understanding and visibility of different types of personal data which will further help to take appropriate actions to establish policies and procedures to protect the data.

37. Answer: (a)

    There are encryption techniques that enable computing on encrypted data without decrypting it in order to provide encryption in-use, meaning that personal data can remain confidential while it is used. Such techniques are widely used and adopted when sharing personal data with another entity (in this scenario, three vendors), where the receiving entity does not need to read or access the (plain) personal data which might otherwise jeopardise the confidentiality of data.

38. Answer: (c)

    There are three major types of privacy governance models, namely centralised, decentralised (also referred to as local), and hybrid. In a centralised model, usually one entity or person is responsible for privacy-related matters. In a decentralised model, the top tier business owners (e.g., executives) within an organisation delegate their privacy-related decision-making authority to lower tiers to bear responsibility for privacy and data protection matters within their scope of operations. The hybrid is a combination of both models.

39. Answer: (b)

    There are multiple aspects that need to be considered when deciding on a work-from-anywhere security policy which includes a diverse range of activities such as level of remote accesses to an organisation's resources and infrastructure, the type of devices that can be used to access resources (e.g. personal devices conditioned on a BYOD policy), the type of resources that can be remotely accessed (e.g., only non-sensitive data) and many more. Thus, this indicates that organisations should make their own risk-based decisions about creating a work-from-anywhere security policy.

40. Answer: (a)

    It is a known practice to allow employees to connect their personal devices to an organisation's network. However, given the fact that many of these devices may not be secure (to the same degree as the organisation's devices), they contribute considerable risk if not managed appropriately. One solution to handle the risk is to create and establish a separate network within an organisation's network which is dedicated only to these devices. Although other options might be helpful to minimise the risk of such devices, they are not completely mitigating the risk. Hence, option (a) seems more likely to do so.

41. Answer: (c)

Except (c), all the other options are examples of recommended practice for password policies. Password hints can guide an intruder to more easily guess someone else's password which eventually makes passwords ineffective against unauthorised access to an organisation's resources.

42. Answer: (d)

Using an email client software (e.g., Microsoft Outlook) by an employee or a user of a system does not require full privileges. This is normally an expected behaviour by a user account (e.g., an employee being able to send/receive emails to/from customers). Such accounts that mainly deal with daily tasks should be set up to have limited privileges. All other options are examples of tasks carried out by an administrative account that often require full privileges.

43. Answer: (a)

Only (a) is an example of a threat (leaving an organisation's laptop unattended) that may result in unauthorised physical access (e.g., someone walking up to the laptop and impersonating an employee or accessing confidential information stored on the laptop).

44. Answer: (a)

Simply relying on consent as a lawful processing basis for personal data sharing activities does not seem to be a an effective way to ensure personal data sharing decisions are handled appropriately. Personal data sharing is a critical aspect of every personal data processing activity carried out by an organisation. Hence, appropriate review processes such as DPIAs can help to evaluate the legitimacy, benefits and risks of a data sharing. Documenting sharing decisions can also help an organisation to demonstrate compliance. It is also highly crucial to ensure employees involved in personal data sharing decisions receive appropriate training and are aware of their responsibilities.

45. Answer: (d)

Although it is good practice to set up a directory of data sharing agreements, limiting this only to active data sharing agreements does not seem to be a reasonable decision. In fact, such a repository should contain all relevant data sharing agreements (both active and passive/inactive) to support an organisation in audit, monitoring and investigation processes.

46. Answer: (b)

When completing a DPIA, it is important to seek advice from the DPO and relevant privacy stakeholders across an organisation. A DPIA should clearly demonstrate all the relevant considerations on the scope and nature of the proposed data processing. This may often conflict with business needs, and thus, incorporating senior-level managers' advice in a DPIA does not seem to be a reasonable approach.

47. Answer: (c)

    Inspecting the compliance of a vendor with an organisation's policies
    and controls at fixed intervals is not good practice. Inspection should
    take place depending on a specific risk assessment strategy that closely
    monitors the deviation of the vendor from compliance requirements.

48. Answer: (c)

    When transferring data off an organisation, a secure form of transport
    should be used. Using a secure public network does not seem to count
    as a secure form of transport as public networks are often vulnerable
    to attacks. As such, other forms such as a Virtual Private Network
    (VPN) or secure courier are recommended.

49. Answer: (a)

    Data quality ensures that personal data stored by an organisation is
    accurate and not excessive.

50. Answer: (b)

    When determining the requirements for a retention policy, it is impor-
    tant to pay attention to both business needs (for what purposes do
    you need to store personal data? How long would be enough to store
    such data to serve the specified purposes? Etc.) and statutory require-
    ments (if you store financial transactions, you may need to comply
    with national and/or international requirements and legislations with
    regard to such data processing activities that often require longer than
    usual retention periods).

51. Answer: (a)

The opposite of (a) is correct (setting up minimum password complexity rules). In other words, organisations should encourage their employees and anyone accessing their resources to follow a minimum password complexity rule (combination of upper/lowercase letters, numbers, and special characters).

52. Answer: (a)

All are examples of privacy dark patterns except (a). (a) is indeed well-aligned with the transparency principle as it shows a big pop-up window to encourage users to read the privacy notice of the website upon the first visit. In short, dark patterns try to manipulate or heavily influence individuals to make certain choices which often go against their interest or will.

53. Answer: (d)

This is an example of inappropriate remote/home working policy that does not limit employees to follow certain procedures when taking devices, data or software off the premises of an organisation. Note that physical security policy is only relevant when the goal is to avoid unauthorised access to physical premises of an organisation. It is already assumed in this question that there is an authorised access (employees taking devices, data or software off the premises of an organisation) to the physical premises of an organisation.

54. Answer: (d)

Business continuity refers to the ability of an organisation to maintain normal operations following any disruptions (e.g., a security incident).

Note that option (a) refers to *business resiliency* which is defined as the ability of an organisation to anticipate, respond, and adapt itself to potential disruptions. Business resiliency is a more broader term than business continuity that encompasses both continuity and recovery aspects of a business following a disruption.

55. Answer: (a)

When examining an individual access request, an organisation shall not get away from the obligation to provide the requested personal data by deleting or modifying personal data in response to a request for access. In this scenario, the organisation notices that at the same time an individual has submitted a data access request, unlawful processing of the individual's job application data is being carried out (as the organisation has stored the data beyond the retention period). Hence, the organisation needs to fulfil the individual's access request and delete the job application data that it holds as it is stored unlawfully (beyond the retention period). As good practice and to avoid a subsequent request for data deletion, the organisation could add information about the reason and time of the deletion.

56. Answer: (c)

When a breach is likely to result in high risks to individuals, notification to supervisory authorities is often required as soon as an organisation becomes aware of the breach (no matter if the investigations have not yet kicked off or detailed information is not yet available).

57. Answer: (b)

It is often recommended to use multiple channels for communicating privacy notices to users, e.g., in-app and via email.

58. Answer: (b)

This is an example of at-setup privacy notices where users are given the option to accept or decline a permission request upon the installation.

59. Answer: (b)

The EU GDPR requires organisations to keep a record of processing activities (known as ROPA) in relation to their data processing activities. ROPA helps an organisation to demonstrate compliance which needs to be provided to a supervisory authority upon request.

60. Answer: (d)

Phishing attacks aim at manipulating or encouraging individuals to do certain actions that may be in the interest of the attacker (e.g., clicking on an infected attachment to redirect a user to a fake banking website controlled by the attacker that looks like a legit website and asking users to enter their credentials while all the information being entered by the user is being captured by the attacker).

61. Answer: (c)

Location of the attacker is not of relevancy when deciding on the impact of a cyber attack on an organisation. Other factors such as affected data types (is it only non-personal data affected or has the attack affected personal data as well?), number of impacted customers (has the attack only affected a few customers or thousands of them?), and availability of services (has the attack led to the disruption of normal operations and services within the organisation?).

62. Answer: (a)

Complex credentials such as complex passwords and usernames indeed play a key role in protecting an organisation against cyber attacks and incidents.

63. Answer: (a)

An incident response plan always requires involvement and alignment of different stakeholders within an organisation such as legal, IT, finance, senior management, and more. Note than an incident response plan is an internal strategy that organisations need to establish and execute which does not require approval from an independent entity such as a supervisory authority.

64. Answer: (c)

Although a ransomware attack is likely to affect multiple security principles, the impact on availability may be huge, especially in cases where the attack contributes to the loss of timely access to personal data which can get even more critical if backups are not available.

65. Answer: (a)

In every privacy training programme it is important to consider both staff and trainers needs. Dedicated resources are vital as well to ensure training is delivered effectively. In addition, timescales are important. In fact, training strategies shall meet training needs within agreed timescales. This helps organisations react briskly as privacy, data protection, and governance landscape and their requirements are evolving quickly. Hence, it is important to determine precise timescales when delivering such training.

66. Answer: (c)

An incident often refers to something bad happening at an organisation. However, it does not always mean that a data breach has occurred. For instance, an organisation suffering from a denial of service attack is experiencing an incident as no breach has occurred. But if any exfiltration would occur, then this might be deemed as a data breach. However, note that a breach might be even broader than exfiltration of personal data. For instance, under the EU GDPR a "personal data breach means a breach of security leading to the accidental or unlawful destruction, loss, alteration, unauthorised disclosure of, or access to, personal data transmitted, stored or otherwise processed". Therefore, exfiltration or data leakage is not the only consideration that should be made when determining if a personal data breach has occurred. Another example is when an organisation fails to have timely access to the personal data (e.g., due to a ransomware attack encrypting data, similar to this scenario). This can be considered as a personal data breach (which is also a security incident in the first place) because the organisation has lost access to personal data.

67. Answer: (d)

Disaster recovery as a control for an incident response plan can help an organisation to ensure if the incident response plan is efficient. Breach notification also involves controls that guarantee how the organisation responds to an incident that has contributed to a breach. Software testing is also an integral part of every incident response plan to identify vulnerabilities in software artefacts and fix them accordingly.

68. Answer: (b)

Identity theft is a type of threat where an attacker uses someone else's personal information (such as usernames and passwords) without their permission to commit criminal activities. Given the fact that many users reuse the same usernames and passwords across online services, identity theft is more likely to occur in this scenario.

69. Answer: (c)

Cost of regulatory fines is not influential when deciding on the implementation of technical and organisational measures to address privacy and security risks within an organisations. In fact, when assessing factors to implement technical and organisational measures to address privacy and security risks, an organisation should be mindful of the severity and likelihood of those risks as well as the cost of implementation of those measures that fight against risks.

70. Answer: (c)

For a consent to be explicit, it shall be expressed explicitly by the user. Option (c) is the most explicit type of consent expression.

71. Answer: (c)

The four well-known authentication factors are: What you know, what you have, what you are, and where you are.

72. Answer: (b)

Designing privacy user interfaces and notices requires to put users' needs and requirements front and centre. It is worth mentioning that, while there are some focus on business and compliance requirements, most privacy design decisions are informed by users' needs and expectations as the ultimate goal of user-centred design is to build products and features with maximum desirability, usability, and usefulness.

73. Answer: (c)

   If the hacked VPN account had a multi-factor authentication, then this might be more likely to prevent the attack. Option (d) can be also considered as a plausible option, however, remember that even strong passwords might be breached, and thus, leaving the whole system without appropriate protection.

74. Answer: (c)

   Except (c), all other options are correct. The attack clearly demonstrates that Company ABC does not have a strong password hygiene policy in place. Such a policy ensures that strong passwords are managed and maintained across an organisation. Improving workforce cyber awareness and training programme is one way to ensure password hygiene policy is met. Finally, the attack has primarily targetted the company's VPN which could potentially be prevented if the company's incident monitoring programme was able to detect events like suspicious use of VPNs, policy invasions, and password abuse.

75. Answer: (c)

   It is good practice for an organisation to run phishing simulation campaigns (from time to time) to evaluate the effectiveness of their education and awareness programme.

76. Answer: (d)

    Cybersecurity threats are often closer to home than one thinks. As an example of this are phishing emails with infected attachments that provide low-hanging fruit for attackers to exploit a system. An efficient intrusion detection system as well as a robust employee cybersecurity awareness programme can help reduce the risk of such attacks.

77. Answer: (c)

    Anonymization allows to remove the association between a database and an individual. Pseudonymization removes the association with an individual and adds an association between a particular set of characteristics relating to that individual and one or more pseudonyms that represent that individual.

78. Answer: (a)

    Regulatory needs dictate the requirements that need to be met when designing consent settings and options for children. Age is also important as most jurisdictions consider individuals under 18 as children and/or minors, however, they may mandate additional requirements when targeting services at children under 13. The presentation of UIs and the way the settings are presented and structured is also another important aspect.

79. Answer: (b)

    Under the HIPAA, an organisation has to respond to an individual's request for access to their data no later than 30 days.

80. Answer: (d)

    CPRA recognises the right to the restriction of sensitive data usage, while CCPA does not. Only CPRA recognises the right to data rectification and the right to rejection of automated decision making (options (a) and (b) are incorrect). None of these two legislations mandates the appointment of DPO (option (c) is incorrect).

81. Answer: (c)

    (a) is incorrect, because a well-known vendor with a bad reputation for compliance is certainly not what an organisation would want. Options (b) and (d) are not entirely incorrect, however, option (c) is more accurate. An organisation needs to establish procedures to confirm that vendors follow their rules. In other words, organisations shall make sure that provisions for information privacy and security (e.g., evaluating and updating information privacy and security controls) are in vendor contracts.

82. Answer: (c)

    Both rights are recognised under the EU GDPR.

83. Answer: (b)

    Right to access to personal data is a widely recognised right under many privacy regimes such as the EU GDPR. Generally speaking, for more than one copy of personal data requested by an individual, an organisation may be able to charge a reasonable fee, and therefore, this indicates that option (a) is incorrect. Every individual whose personal data is held by organisations is entitled to this right (option (c) is incorrect). Exceptions may apply to children under 13 who may not be able to exercise this right themselves, rather their parents or guardians. This right is not for granted, meaning that under some circumstances where the request is manifestly unfounded or excessive, an organisation may decline the request.

84. Answer: (d)

    According to Article 28 (4) of the GDPR, if the sub-processor fails to fulfil its data protection obligations, "the initial processor shall remain fully liable to the controller for the performance of that other processor's obligations".

85. Answer: (d)

    (d) does not refer to the data minimisation principle, rather the purpose limitation principle.

86. Answer: (a)

    Disclosing the information of customers for special meal offers would be incompatible with the purposes for which the data was collected for, and thus, (a) is the correct answer. Option (b) goes against the the data minimisation principle (not purpose limitation) as it would be irrelevant and excessive to obtain such information from an individual who was applying for a non-manual occupation. Options (c) and (d) are incorrect as well, because they do not refer to purpose limitation principle.

87. Answer: (c)

Off-chance collection of personal data (we collect it now, and we will see if this is going to be useful or relevant in the future) is strictly discouraged by the data minimisation principle. The health service provider only collects the blood groups of a selected number of staff who do hazardous work (not all the staff).

88. Answer: (c)

(c) is more relevant as if such a database stores incorrect/outdated data, an individual is going to be more likely to suffer negative effects (having a credit application rejected due to inaccurate credit history information).

89. Answer: (b)

The goal of the Privacy Maturity Model (PMM) is to serve as a benchmark for organisations, so that they could assess and measure the progress of a their privacy programme. This way, an organisation is provided with a comparative instrument to evaluate the status of its privacy initiatives across its stakeholders and/or (inter)national units.

90. Answer: (d)

The number of meetings held by privacy teams within an organisation does not necessarily tell anything about the efficiency of a privacy programme (some employees or teams may be more or less in the favour of frequent meetings, no matter what those meetings may entail). Number of personal data breaches clearly tells a lot about how mature and efficient a privacy programme is. The rate of consent for personal data sharing is interesting as individual's rights could be used as metrics to assess the overall progress of a privacy programme. For instance, if an organisation observes a dramatic descending trend in opt-out of personal data sharing by its users (e.g., following a privacy scandal), then this information might be useful to evaluate users' trust in the privacy programme and how well it protects their privacy. Number of signed transfer impact assessments can also be considered as a metric as failing to successfully initiate these agreements may result in huge regulatory scrutiny and/or fines.

Made in United States
Troutdale, OR
02/04/2024

17346424R10086